ENTRY OF YOUNG PEOPLE INTO WORKING LIFE

GENERAL REPORT

ORGANISATION FOR ECONOMIC CO-OPERATION AND DEVELOPMENT

The Organisation for Economic Co-operation and Development (OECD) was set up under a Convention signed in Paris on 14th December, 1960, which provides that the OECD shall promote policies designed:

— to achieve the highest sustainable economic growth and employment and a rising standard of living in Member countries, while maintaining financial stability, and thus to contribute to the development of the world economy;
— to contribute to sound economic expansion in Member as well as non-member countries in the process of economic development;
— to contribute to the expansion of world trade on a multilateral, non-discriminatory basis in accordance with international obligations.

The Members of OECD are Australia, Austria, Belgium, Canada, Denmark, Finland, France, the Federal Republic of Germany, Greece, Iceland, Ireland, Italy, Japan, Luxembourg, the Netherlands, New Zealand, Norway, Portugal, Spain, Sweden, Switzerland, Turkey, the United Kingdom and the United States.

* *

CONTENTS

Part Two

CURRENT RESPONSES TO YOUTH UNEMPLOYMENT

LIST OF TABLES

GRAPH

FOREWORD

The first part of this report examines the problems of the transition from school to work. The second part analyses the measures undertaken in various countries in order to deal with youth unemployment.

The Secretariat wished to acknowledge the help received from Dr. Beatrice G. Reubens, Senior Research Associate, University of Columbia, New York, for the preparation of the second part.

In preparing the present publication the Secretariat drew heavily on a series of technical reports prepared to this end by the national authorities or individual experts in the Member countries. These reports are published separately under the title Entry of Young People into Working Life - Technical Reports.

This report is published under the responsibility of the Secretary General and does not necessarily commit Member governments to all the views expressed in it.

PREFACE

The social and economic development of the industrialised countries over the last thirty years has been accompanied by new preoccupations and priorities in education and employment policies. Such policies have always been inter-related, although education has tended to develop somewhat autonomously over the last twenty years in response to rising socio-cultural demands which it was possible to meet in this period of rapid economic growth. The emphasis was in fact on the satisfaction of social demand for education and the reduction of social inequalities, including better opportunities of access for the less favoured social groups. At the same time, the continued expansion of economic activity and the development of productive services meant that an acceptable balance between employment supply and demand could be maintained at all levels.

Over and above conjunctural problems, the present crisis among Western nations seems to coincide with changes in the structures of growth. Changes in productivity and in the shape of the age pyramid in employment corresponding to the increase in social demand tend to lead to longer term imbalances between the growing demand for employment and the absorptive capacity of the economy. For these reasons policies for full employment will probably call for a built-in policy for job creation, in order to absorb the different categories of those seeking employment with minimum social strain. In other words, both educational qualifications and personal aspirations must be taken into account.

Within this context, the situation of young people is revealing in many respects. Its very diversity makes it a representative example of the problems which will have to be faced in the near future. Young people have, by definition, benefited to the greatest extent from the expansion of the education system. At a very early age, they have been exposed to modern methods of information which open up the world outside. They have had considerably better living standards than earlier generations and this has led them to be both culturally and materially more demanding. Since social policy tends, for very good reasons, to give priority to protecting adults with family responsibilities, the younger generation has felt the saturation effects of certain employment sectors most forcibly. Young

7

people can more easily than others be given training which allows them to move into new jobs corresponding to present and po ential needs of final demand. These are the ideas and the background which underlie the present analysis of the entry of young people into working life. Educational and the employment perspectives are looked at jointly, together with the needs of other categories of people seeking employment, such as adults or women who are the subject of other OECD activities.

The first part, which is based on data collected by the Member countries and, in particular, on country reports provided by about a dozen of them, gives an analytical picture of young people's difficulties in entering working life; a number of categories, based on the type of vocational training received, are identified. There follows a brief description of the way in which the expansion of the education system has affected the volume and kind of demand for employment. The various situations which young people face in their studies and their search for a job are compared with the realities of the world of work with some reference to attitudinal problems.

The first aspect leads to an examination of the vocational and professional validity of the different kinds of training available to young people, the links between school and work, information services, whether in school or not, which are available to candidates applying for a job, and the limits imposed on the absorptive capacity by present economic structures. Attitudinal aspects involve such practices as conditioning young people's choices and their future prospects; examples are attitudes within the educational system, attitudes to be found among employers, in private or public enterprises and those reflected by the hierarchy of salaries. Moreover, the aspirations of young people may or may not coincide with the socio-economic rationale and realities.

In Part II the measures taken in various countries to deal with the young unemployed are examined. After looking briefly at youth unemployment in the wider context of employment in general and the effect on young people of general measures taken against unemployment, the analysis focusses in greater detail on those measures which concern young people more specifically. To this end the report presents a typology, which groups under six headings the fifteen different categories of measures which have been identified.

The signficance of these measures is examined within the general framework described at the beginning of this preface. They are looked at from the point of view of their possible convergence, inasmuch as they are intended in some cases to deal with conjunctural problems and in others to help young people to enter satisfactorily into working life with good career prospects.

Part One

PROBLEMS OF TRANSITION
FROM SCHOOL TO WORKING LIFE

INTRODUCTION

In most countries there was a rise in the birth rate after the Second World War and the increase in the number of young people became a matter of concern for the education authorities. The effect on employment was somewhat delayed because young people tended to remain longer in the educational system. It was not therefore immediately obvious that there was no corresponding increase in the number of employment opportunities.

It now appears that recruitment or employment opportunities and the types of education provided or the aspirations of young people do not always coincide. Moreover the recent economic recession has widened the gap and the entry of young people into working life has become an acute problem.

The problem is not a simple one of reconciling supply and demand. It involves the personal development of young people and the ways in which they make the transition from school to working life. Their entry into working life, far from being a marginal aspect of the employment situation, is the central mechanism by which the work force is renewed.

The first part of this report sets out to investigate the passage from school to work within the wider context of the socialisation of young people. Entry into working life marks the moment at which young people normally assume responsibility for their own conduct.

This first part looks at the reasons why it has become difficult to integrate young people into working life. These include the nature of the education and training provided by the school system, the lack of adequate guidance and counselling about jobs, transitional problems and the relatively rigid employment structures. This analysis concludes with a series of proposals designed to reduce some of the imbalances that lie at the root of the problem.

In Part II the various cyclical measures which have been adopted by governments to reduce youth unemployment are considered. Special attention will be paid to the extent to which these measures accord with the requirements of long-term strategies for dealing with structural employment problems.

The present investigation shows how young people, in different ways and degrees, as well as other less privileged social groups, are faced with difficult problems of a continuing nature for which solutions should be found within the framework of overall social policies. Indeed, if the generation gap is not to be aggravated it seems essential to avoid formulating policies which treat the young as a separate social group.

The situation of young people illustrates rather well the contemporary dilemma of the individual set against the social and economic system. It is hardly surprising that young people should be peculiarly sensitive to this dilemma. Many of them question and even reject the values which seem to underlie school, work and society in general. Education should therefore help them to develop critical ideas and attitudes which are at the same time constructive. In more general terms both education and employment policies should aim to maximise individual freedom within the economic system and to encourage individuals to bring their best contribution to the general good.

The analysis does not deal in detail with the present situation in every country since statistical data are fragmentary and do not permit comparisons to be made between countries. However, the analysis endeavours to reflect certain fundamental trends and changes in modern societies. The material contained in ten national reports(1) on the entry of young people into working life has provided a unique source of information from which to derive some general ideas and conclusions.

---

1) The list of these national reports is given in the Bibliography. They are published under the title "Entry of Young People into Working Life - Technical Reports".

I. THE PROBLEM

There is a general awareness of the youth employment problem but the extent to which young people themselves are conscious of facing difficulties is not clear. Not all of them fail to find jobs; not all of them feel that the jobs they obtain do not come up to their expectations. For this reason, it is useful to devise a typology of young people in relation to their entry into employment.

Entry into working life is not normally a once and for all affair but a process extending from compulsory education to settling into a more or less permanent job. In some countries, for many young people, the opportunity of combining work with education makes the transition from school to employment less abrupt. The process of transition considered here may well cover many years - for example, from the age of 16 to 25 or even 30.

The diversity of national situations makes the development of a typology extremely difficult. In some countries, such as the United States and Canada, the development of education complicates the analysis. In the United States in particular, the educational choices made by young people seem to adjust fairly rapidly to employment trends and graduates seem more willing to accept the jobs available. In other countries, where there has been a continuing process of more balanced economic growth, as in Spain or Germany, attention is drawn to specific problems of some categories of youth. In Germany and Austria, a large majority of young people obtain vocational training in the eduational system or in enterprises. In Italy, attention is at present focussed on the difficulties of university graduates in finding employment. In Japan, the special character of employment means that employers prefer to employ young people. In the Scandinavian countries, which are experiencing a relatively favourable employment situation, attention is centred around the problems of qualitative adaptation. The typology presented below may therefore seem overly influenced by the situation in certain European countries. However, it is more useful for the analysis and examination of the different national situations to emphasize the similarities rather than the differences.

A typology of young people in relation to employment includes among others the criteria of age, sex and level of education.

As to the age criterion, it seems that unemployment rates among young people are in inverse proportion to age. Employers often hesitate to take on young people without experience, especially when they also lack a useable skill. At the same time, young people with a high level of education may deliberately spend a long time in searching for a job that they consider suitable. Thus, while there can be no doubt that the very young, who are unqualified or relatively unqualified, are at a disadvantage in finding a job, young people from widely varied backgrounds find themselves in similar situations. The higher rates of unemployment which exist among girls seem to be due to the fact that they have greater difficulty than boys in finding their first job.

In Europe the determining criterion - even in periods of expanding economic activity - would appear to be the nature of the educational and occupational training received. This criterion allows a typology of young people entering the work force to be formulated as follows:

i) Those leaving compulsory school with no vocational training and possibly a sense of educational failure must resign themselves to the lowest levels of employment and they have limited prospects of promotion. They are often against the idea of training courses, especially when these are labelled "education".

ii) Those who have undergone basic occupational training, either within the education system or through Ministry of Labour programmes, are in a slightly more favourable position. They often find themselves eligible, however, only for unskilled or low-skilled jobs and, like the previous group, they encounter much job instability.

iii) Those who become apprentices or who benefit in some large enterprises from quasi-apprenticeship status have reasonable prospects. Although there is much criticism of apprenticeship it does seem to provide a better induction into the world of work.

iv) Those who have undergone a solid occupational training as highly-skilled craftsmen or technicians meet with little difficulty in finding a job, although they may have to change jobs in order to earn higher pay. However, the certificates acquired by some technicians, especially in the services sector, are not highly regarded by employers. This is because the training upon which they are based does not always relate to specific occupational functions.

v) Those who follow general secondary education courses are widely distributed throughout the occupational hierarchy. The most fortunate go into services such as banks, for example, where careers are secure and salaries good. Others may have to be content with less satisfactory jobs or face unemployment. A large number try to acquire a middle-level vocational training.

vi) The prospects of those who graduate from higher education institutions mainly depend upon whether or not they have followed professional courses. Those who have followed professional courses as a rule find jobs, although frequently at a level below their expectations. Those with general degrees who cannot obtain a job in the public sector often find themselves little better off than those who have completed their secondary education.

It is difficult to place young people who follow part-time courses in this typology. In general, they are better off than those who follow full-time courses, at least at the beginning of their careers. Another category of young people who are difficult to place in the typology are those who drop out without acquiring a qualification. Their career prospects vary according to the level of their educational attainment and the sector of employment which they enter. More detailed statistical information about these two categories is required before they can be placed accurately in the typology.

Some general conclusions can be drawn from the analysis. In the first place, those who continue their studies after the end of compulsory schooling, especially up to the higher education level, are normally at an advantage; they benefit, especially in Europe, from the existing employment structure which reflects the division of society into social and occupational strata.

It may also be noted that those who have received no more than a general education at any level face problems in obtaining employment even during a period of high economic growth. The great majority are obliged to take low paid jobs with poor promotion prospects. By contrast, those who have acquired a vocational qualification, either through the educational system or apprenticeship, secure employment relatively easily - employment which is, as a rule, satisfying, even though the remuneration paid to skilled manual workers and technicians may be felt to be insufficient. This general rule may apply less in the United States, where it would seem that those who have acquired occupational training at the secondary level do not derive any marked benefit from it.

Finally, the prevailing widespread malaise among young people, which is a relatively new phenomenon, reinforces the need for policy measures to facilitate their entry into active life on social as well as economic grounds.

II. THE TRANSITION

Problems associated with the transition from school to work are
more acute in some countries than in others. They are determined by
a variety of factors which will now be examined, with a summary of
the relevant opinions and studies - in particular those referred to
in the national reports.

A. EMPLOYMENT AND SCHOOLING

The aim here is to present a general picture of the situation
of young people, to describe the training and employment options
available to them, and to identify the factors which influence their
choices.

1. The young in relation to the working population

The expansion of education over the last few decades, which has
been achieved largely by prolonging the period of compulsory and post-
compulsory schooling (see Tables 1 and 2), has had the obvious effect
of raising the level of education of the younger generation vis-à-vis
the working population as a whole (see Table 3 for the United States
and Table 4 for France).

Table 1

COMPULSORY EDUCATION IN OECD COUNTRIES

Country	Age of Entry	Age of Exit	Duration (in years)
Australia	6	15-16	9-10
Austria	6	15	9
Belgium	6	14	8
Canada	6	15-16	9-10
Denmark	7	16	9
Finland	7	16	9
France	6	16	10
Germany	6	15	9
Greece	$5\frac{1}{2}$	$11\frac{1}{2}$	6
Iceland	7	15	8
Ireland	6	15	9
Italy	6	14	8
Japan	6	15	9
Luxembourg	6	15	9
Netherlands	6	15	9
New Zealand	6	15	9
Norway	7	16	9
Portugal	7	14	8
Spain	6	14	8
Sweden	7	16	9
Switzerland	6-7	14-16	8-9
Turkey	7	12	5
United Kingdom	5	16	11
United States	6	16	10
Yugoslavia	7	15	8

Source: OECD, Educational Statistics Yearbook, 1974, Vol. 1, Table 1,
        updated for New Zealand and United States.

Table 2

FULL-TIME ENROLMENT RATES OF 15-25 YEAR OLDS(1)

		15	16	17	18	19	20	21	22	23	24	25
Australia	1971	81.5	54.2	37.2	23.6	n.a.	n.a.	n.a.	n.a.	n.a.	n.a.	n.a.
Austria	1969	54.8	32.6	23.6	16.4	10.4	8.7	7.5	6.7	5.6	4.5	4.4
Belgium	1966	75.1	61.3	47.0	33.2	24.4	16.9	13.0	7.3	5.2	3.4	3.4
Canada	1970	98.0	89.1	77.2	45.8	31.6	25.9	21.0	12.6	8.3	5.5	n.d.
Denmark	1970	85.2	66.8	31.8	23.2	18.0	14.7	14.8	14.6	12.5	10.9	4.3
Finland	1967	(59.2)	51.9	43.5	35.2	26.9	20.7	19.0	17.9	16.7	14.2	9.5
France	1970	80.5	62.6	45.1	29.1	19.5	16.2	15.6	12.9	9.7	6.5	11.6
Germany	1969	54.9	30.8	20.4	15.7	12.6	10.6	9.5	9.1	7.5	6.9	6.9
Greece	1969	56.3	49.1	45.8	26.1	(20.7)	(20.1)	(18.6)	(7.6)	6.7	4.9	5.8
Ireland	1973	77.1	60.9	44.2	22.2	13.5	10.0	7.0	7.0	3.0	1.5	3.7
Italy	1966	42.1	33.6	27.4	20.2	15.5		11.2	4.5	(1.1)	(0.2)	n.d.
Japan	1970	(83.8)	(79.0)	(74.8)	(29.9)	(22.0)	(13.8)	(13.7)	(0.9)	5.4	3.2	n.d.
Luxembourg	1970	56.5	40.5	30.2	22.4	17.8	13.5	11.1	7.2	6.7	5.1	(0.2)
Netherlands	1970	79.7	60.6	41.5	28.4	20.6	15.1	11.1	8.4	14.2	11.4	1.3
Norway	1970	94.2	74.6	59.8	46.5	31.7	22.6	19.5	17.1	6.4	5.4	4.6
Portugal	1970	30.1	25.4	22.0	20.4	16.3	13.0	9.5	7.5	6.4	6.6	n.d.
Spain	1970	35.0	29.6	22.8	19.0	16.7	19.0	11.0	6.7	6.6	6.6	5.7
Sweden	1972	96.7	74.0	60.8	40.8	24.0	19.8	17.9	16.5	13.9	11.8	5.8
Switzerland	1970	95.9	66.7	54.8	32.8	9.0	9.0	5.9	5.4	4.9	11.8	9.6
United Kingdom	1970	73.0	41.5	26.2	17.6	14.3	12.4		4.6		4.2	3.5
United States	1970	97.7	93.5	86.2	53.8	40.9	(35.4)	(28.3)		14.9	n.d.	n.d.

1) Figures in brackets are estimates.

Source: Yearbook of Educational Statistics, Vol. I., OECD 1974. Tables 16 and 17.
Ireland: M.E.J. O'Kelly, "The Insertion of Youth into Working Life - The Irish Situation", in Entry of Young People into Working Life - Technical Reports (forthcoming), Table 1.

Table 3

UNITED STATES: EDUCATIONAL ATTAINMENT OF THE
ACTIVE CIVIL POPULATION BY AGE GROUP (AVERAGE
NUMBER OF YEARS OF STUDY), 1952 AND 1974

Age group	Males		Females		Together	
	1952	1974	1952	1974	1952	1974
18-24 years	11.5	12.6	12.4	12.7	12.2	12.6
25-34 years	12.1	12.8	12.2	12.7	12.1	12.8
35-44 years	11.2	12.6	11.9	12.5	11.4	12.5
45-54 years	8.7	12.4	9.2	12.4	8.8	12.4
55-64 years		12.1		12.3		12.1
65 years and over	8.2	10.7	8.8	11.1	8.3	10.9
Total	10.4	12.4	10.8	12.5	10.9	12.5

Source: Manpower Report of the President, U.S. Department of Labour,
U.S. Government Printing Offices, Washington 1975, Tables
B-9 and B-11.

At the same time, the number of young people in the work force
has tended to decline, although more recently the tendency appears
to have slowed down and the number has even gone up slightly (Tables
5 and 6 illustrate the trend in the United States and Sweden; in
Ireland the flattening out process is not apparent, Table 7).

It will be seen that girls may often be worse off than boys
either because they leave school earlier or because they take only
general subjects. Being frequently unqualified, they accept low-
grade jobs. In highly developed regions the gap between girls and
boys appears to be narrowing (Table 8 gives a rough indication of
the proportion of girls in post-primary education in Germany and
Italy).

In France, the low enrolment of girls in post-primary public
institutions is counter-balanced by their high enrolment in private
institutions where they receive occupational training (see Table 9).
In this country, when girls do not find the training opportunities
they are looking for in public institutions, they turn to commercial
schools.

The fact that so many girls obtain a vocational training outside the public school system suggests that a more diversified curriculum is required within the system. Despite the trend to equalise
training opportunities for girls and boys[1], many girls are still
inclined to seek employment within a specific range of occupations.

---

1) See in particular on this point the programme carried out within
the OECD by the Manpower and Social Affairs Committee on "The
role of women in the economy".

Table 4

FRANCE: EDUCATIONAL ATTAINMENT OF THE ACTIVE POPULATION IN MARCH 1972

(Percentages)

Levels		15-19	20-24	25-29	30-34	35-39	40-44	45-49	50-54	55-59	60-64	54-69	70-74	75 years and over	Total
No diploma	Men	38.8	21.4	21.1	25.9	33.4	36.1	32.5	32.6	39.1	46.7	49.2	41.4	41.9	31.7
	Women	27.8	18.3	15.8	19.3	28.3	30.9	30.3	35.1	44.3	50.0	54.0	53.9	55.6	28.5
Primary	Men	35.9	21.5	19.2	20.5	23.1	27.5	36.6	36.6	33.9	32.1	31.3	34.6	39.7	27.7
	Women	42.5	24.6	23.5	28.2	32.2	36.5	42.1	38.3	37.4	35.9	35.9	35.2	34.8	32.7
Secondary	Men	24.7	54.2	49.6	43.6	36.1	30.7	24.9	25.1	21.4	15.4	14.0	13.1	11.0	34.2
	Women	29.1	50.4	46.7	41.5	32.6	27.6	23.0	22.5	15.1	11.2	12.4	10.2	9.6	32.3
Post-secondary	Men	0.1	2.0	4.3	2.8	1.6	1.5	1.2	0.9	1.1	0.7	0.3	0.8	–	1.8
	Women	0.1	5.2	7.6	5.2	4.1	2.9	2.9	2.2	1.5	1.5	1.7	0.4	–	3.8
Higher	Men	–	0.7	5.7	7.1	5.7	4.1	4.8	4.7	4.4	5.0	5.1	9.7	7.4	4.5
	Women	0.4	1.4	6.3	5.8	2.8	2.9	1.7	1.9	1.6	1.3	0.6	0.3	–	2.6
Total(1)	Men	100.0	100.0	100.0	100.0	100.0	100.0	100.0	100.0	100.0	100.0	100.0	100.0	100.0	100.0
	Women	100.0	100.0	100.0	100.0	100.0	100.0	100.0	100.0	100.0	100.0	100.0	100.0	100.0	100.0

1) The slight divergencies between the totals and the sums of the individual percentage figures stem from a "Not declared" column.

Derived from: R. Pohl and others, Enquête sur l'emploi de 1972. Les collections de l'INSEE, Démographie et Emploi, No. 33-34, Paris, 1974.

20

Table 5

SWEDEN: PERCENTAGE ACTIVITY RATES BY AGE GROUP, 1965-1974(1)

Age group		1965	1966	1967	1968	1969	1970	1971	1972	1973	1974
16-19	Men	62.2	59.0	53.9	55.1	54.0	52.8	53.7	53.5	53.7	57.1
	Women	57.0	54.7	50.9	54.0	50.6	50.9	51.9	50.4	49.8	53.4
20-24	Men	79.8	79.1	78.2	77.6	77.8	76.7	76.0	76.6	78.4	80.7
	Women	63.6	69.6	62.4	63.6	64.4	65.2	65.8	68.0	67.6	71.1
25-34	Men	95.5	95.2	94.5	94.6	94.6	93.5	94.0	93.2	93.7	94.1
	Women	53.5	52.1	51.7	55.7	58.6	60.7	62.6	63.8	65.0	68.0
35-44	Men	96.8	97.4	96.9	95.6	96.1	96.4	95.4	95.1	95.0	95.7
	Women	57.5	59.5	61.7	63.4	64.6	67.4	69.9	71.2	71.5	74.2
45-54	Men	96.1	96.2	95.4	95.0	94.4	94.8	94.9	94.4	94.3	93.9
	Women	56.8	60.0	59.3	60.2	61.6	65.0	67.7	69.5	71.0	72.7
55-64	Men	88.3	88.4	89.2	89.0	86.6	85.4	84.7	83.5	82.7	82.0
	Women	39.2	42.2	43.5	42.9	44.2	44.5	44.7	45.5	46.3	47.6
65-69	Men	47.2	46.4	45.6	45.8	42.1	40.0	38.0	35.1	32.5	29.0
	Women	15.4	14.7	11.1	14.8	15.9	13.1	12.6	11.9	11.3	9.7
70-74	Men	24.9	20.5	18.5	16.3	16.1	14.0	13.6	13.8	12.5	12.9
	Women	6.8	4.6	4.3	2.5	2.5	3.3	2.5	2.9	2.5	2.3

1) From 1965-1969: means of observations made in February, May, August, and November; from 1970 to 1974: yearly averages.

Source: Statistiska Centralbyrån, Arbetskraftsundersökningen (Labour Force Survey), 1965-1974.

21

Table 6

UNITED STATES: PERCENTAGE ACTIVITY RATES BY AGE GROUP, 1950-1974

Age group		1950	1960	1967	1968	1969	1970	1971	1972	1973	1974
14-15	Men	28.7	22.3	22.0	22.1	22.0	22.1	22.5	22.2	22.8	23.0
	Women	12.7	12.6	14.5	14.8	15.3	16.2	15.9	16.4	17.2	17.4
16-19	Men	63.2	56.1	55.6	55.1	55.9	56.1	56.1	58.1	59.8	60.7
	Women	40.9	39.4	41.6	41.9	43.2	44.0	43.5	45.9	47.8	49.2
20-24	Men	87.8	88.1	84.4	82.7	82.8	83.3	83.0	85.3	85.3	86.0
	Women	46.0	46.1	53.3	54.4	56.7	57.7	57.7	59.0	61.1	63.0
25 +	Men	28.4	85.8	83.3	83.2	82.8	83.6	81.9	81.1	79.2	80.2
	Women	31.6	36.6	39.4	40.2	40.6	41.1	41.1	41.3	41.8	42.5
Together	Men	84.0	80.4	77.0	76.7	76.4	74.8	75.8	75.6	74.6	75.5
	Women	33.1	36.7	39.8	39.8	41.3	41.9	41.9	42.5	43.3	44.2

Derived from: Manpower Report of the President, 1975, op.cit., Table A.3, A.11.

Table 7

IRELAND: PERCENTAGE ACTIVITY RATES BY AGE GROUP, 1961-1971

Age group		1961	1966	1971
14-19	Men	56.2	53.8	43.2
	Women	46.6	46.6	38.6
20-24	Men	90.0	89.4	88.9
	Women	67.2	66.8	65.0

Source: M.J.E. O'Kelly, Insertion of Youth into Working Life,
op.cit., Table 2c.

Table 8

GERMANY AND ITALY: PROPORTION OF GIRLS IN POST-PRIMARY
EDUCATION, 1960-1970

(As % of total for both sexes)

Type of Education	Germany		Italy	
	1960	1969	1960	1970
Compulsory secondary				
Transition	40.9	44.3	41.7	46.7
General terminal	50.4	50.1		
Post-compulsory secondary				
General transition	38.2	39.7	22.9	17.5
Technical transition		47.9	51.5	56.6
General terminal	68.5	52.8	90.0	94.3
Technical terminal	53.3	60.9	33.7	42.5
Higher				
Non-university	7.3	6.7	45.2	49.4
University	20.8	39.8	26.2	38.3

Derived from: Yearbook of Educational Statistics, OECD.

23

Table 9

FRANCE: PROPORTION OF GIRLS IN SECONDARY EDUCATION
(As % of total enrolment) (1965-73)

Education – Stage	1965-1966			1972-1973		
	Public	Private	Total	Public	Private	Total
First cycle (general)	51.1	53.5	51.6	50.5	51.1	50.6
Pre-vocational and preparation for apprenticeship	-	-	-	35.6	47.9	37.4
Short second cycle:						
- general	-	-	-	53.1	73.7	57.0
- vocational	44.2	71.0	52.5	41.8	67.1	48.1
Long second cycle:						
- general	54.6	53.0	54.2	60.8	54.5	59.3
- vocational	37.1	59.9	39.5	37.5	49.3	39.1

Derived from: Note d'information du Ministère de l'Education
Nationale (74-17), dated 3rd May, 1974.

It cannot be inferred from the tables showing school enrolments that there has been a net decrease in the employment of young people since many of them may combine study with paid employment. This practice is becoming more and more common as the statistics from the United States show (Table 10). These statistics should not be interpreted too literally since they may classify those who work for a living with those who simply want to earn a little money. For example, in the United States (see Table 10) many of the young people included in workforce statistics are in fact in seasonal jobs and only work occasionally for a limited number of hours.

Table 10

UNITED STATES: LABOR FORCE PARTICIPATION RATE,
YOUNG PEOPLE ENROLLED IN SCHOOL, 1958 AND 1973

	Age 14-19		Age 20-24	
	1958	1973	1958	1973
1. School enrolment (x 1000)	11,010	18,636	1,308	3,651
2. Number of which in the labour force (x 1000)	2,513	5,880	603	1,933
Percentage (2/1)	22.8	31.8	46.1	52.8

Source: Manpower Report of the President, 1975, Table B-5.

Table 11

UNITED STATES: CIVILIAN LABOUR FORCE BY AGE GROUP, 1955-1974

Age	1955		1960		1965		1970		1974	
	x1000	%	x1000	%	x1000	%	x1000	%	x1000	%
- 18 years	2,535	3.9	3,077	4.4	3,665	4.9	4,661	5.5	5,472	5.9
18 - 19 years	2,382	3.6	2,797	3.9	3,425	4.5	4,114	4.9	5,041	5.4
20 - 24 years	5,666	8.6	6,703	10.9	8,258	10.9	10,583	12.6	13,084	14.1
25 years and over	55,264	83.9	58,085	79.7	60,287	79.7	61,886	77.0	69,115	74.6
Total	65,847	100.0	70,612	100.0	75,635	100.0	84,244	100.0	92,712	100.0

Derived from: Manpower Report of the President, 1975. Tables A-3, A-6.

25

The combined effect of demographic forces and the increasing demand for jobs has brought about a rise in the proportion of young
people in the workforce despite the tendency for them to stay on
longer at school and, until recently, a decline in their activity
rates. Table 11 illustrates this tendency in the United States.

2. Options available to young people

The options available to young people at the upper secondary
stage are extensively discussed in a recent OECD report.(1) However,
since this report deals mainly with educational structures, the present report will focus upon the vocational component in educational
courses and examine which changes in educational structures could
facilitate the transition from school to work.

One of the initial characteristics of educational expansion was
the development of general education at the expense of vocational
and technical courses. This occurred partly because of the growing
demand for the former in binary systems, because of the increasing
preeminence of academic courses in comprehensive schools, for example, in Sweden and the United States, and partly because many students found it easier to obtain access to upper secondary courses
not directly related to a vocational outlet (for example, the "open"
sector in Sweden, the universities in France as opposed to the
"grandes écoles"). The tendency for young people to follow academic
rather than vocational courses is no doubt influenced by the value
system prevailing in many schools, and also by the role played by a
classical education in meritocratic societies. In very recent years,
however, the growth of graduate unemployment has led in certain
countries to a revival of interest in vocationally-oriented courses
(see Tables 12 and 13).

Table 12

FRANCE: COMPARISON OF THE GENERAL AND TECHNICAL
BACCALAUREATS OVER THE YEARS 1970-1973

(Percentages)

Baccalauréats	1970	1971	1972	1973
General	80.6	79.9	78.5	76.7
Technical	19.4	20.1	21.5	23.3
Total	100.0	100.0	100.0	100.0

Source: Le Monde de la Technologie, May 1974.

1) Beyond Compulsory Schooling: Options and changes in upper secondary education, OECD, Paris, 1976.

Table 13

SWEDEN: NEW ENTRANTS IN UNIVERSITY-TYPE HIGHER EDUCATION, 1960-1975

Faculty/institute	60/61	65/66	70/71	71/72	72/73	73/74[1]	74/75[2]
Medicine	453	718	976	976	1,026	1,026	1,026
Technology	1,056	2,153	3,187	3,277	3,352	3,427	3,452
Business administration	345	725	275	275	275	275	275
Odontology	240	260	360	380	440	500	500
Pharmacy	260	320	320	320	240	160	160
Forestry	36	36	40	40	40	40	40
Agriculture	46	65	105	105	105	105	105
Veterinary	30	40	50	50	50	50	50
Gymnastics teacher training	70	150	225	225	250	250	250
Social services	265	630	1,635	1,905	1,995	1,995	1,995
Journalism	–	150	240	240	240	240	240
	–	20	25	40	400	400	400
Total restricted intake capacity	2,801	5,267	7,458	7,833	8,413	8,468	8,493
Total restricted new entrants	1,963	3,594	4,642	5,304	5,351	5,603	5,600
Law	436	877	1,118	1,464	1,253	1,273	1,300
Humanities and Theology	3,869	5,337	6,846	5,351	5,636	5,429	5,700
Social Sciences	1,535	4,858	11,064	8,304	7,729	7,820	8,900
Natural Sciences		2,915	3,605	2,700	2,676	2,269	2,300
Total unrestricted faculties	5,840	13,987	22,633	17,815	17,294	16,791	18,100
Total	7,803	17,581	27,275	23,125	22,645	22,394	23,700

1) Provisional figures.
2) Forecast.

Source: Office of the Chancellor of the Swedish Universities.

The result is that many types of education - such as general secondary school education - which are conceived as a transition to, and preparation for, higher education, in effect assume a terminal character for the vast majority of pupils, and generally speaking a large number of young people find themselves on the labour market, sometimes after long years of study, without any marketable skill.(1)

One solution to this problem would appear to be to provide contacts with working life at an earlier stage. But this solution is not easy to apply for at least three reasons.

First, it is difficult to provide meaningful work experiences for young people during the period of initial training. Experience with trainees in France, apprentices in Germany and with sandwich courses in the United Kingdom shows that only a limited number of people can usefully be accommodated at the workplace at any given time. The general adoption of work/study schemes would entail overcoming the current structural limitations on suitable placements.

Secondly, it often happens that because trainees necessarily start without a skill, they are given unskilled tasks to perform instead of tasks which complement their theoretical studies. The fact is that in order to profit from work/study combinations trainees need to receive an initial basic training so that when they enter the workplace they can start at once on a job which will enable them to acquire the desired occupational competence.

Thirdly, work/study combinations may be more appropriate for some training processes than others. They are perhaps most useful in those trades where it is possible to start at the bottom and progress towards the top. There is at present little evidence on this point, and it clearly requires further investigation.

A major consequence of the expansion of education has been its effect on apprenticeship. In many countries apprenticeship used to be a privileged means of acquiring occupational skills. It was also an effective means of inducting young people without academic ambitions into adult life. In the recent past there has been a marked decrease in the volume of apprenticeship. Table 14 shows the declining trend in France. It should be noted, however, that there now appears to be a slight revival of apprenticeship programmes.

In addition to the occupational training provided by schools and the apprenticeship system, the public authorities frequently offer formal training programmes. In some countries, e.g. Italy, these programmes represent the bulk of occupational training for school leavers. Moreover, some young people take full advantage of ad hoc courses intended for workers of all ages, especially during periods of economic recession.

---

1) See Selection and Certification in Education and Employment, OECD, Paris (forthcoming).

Table 14

FRANCE: NUMBER OF APPRENTICES AND YOUNG WORKERS UNDERGOING
VOCATIONAL TRAINING COURSES, 1968-1973

School year	1st year	2nd year	3rd year	Beyond the 3rd year	Total
Boys					
1968-69	54,648	71,289	88,889	4,878	214,714
1969-70	64,922	62,969	68,983	4,165	201,039
1970-71	69,797	69,857	58,165	2,435	200,254
1971-72	59,525	72,931	62,547	2,463	197,460
1972-73	44,126	58,675	51,207	1,149	155,157
Girls					
1968-69	21,428	23,942	25,919	1,596	72,885
1969-70	24,124	21,567	21,450	919	68,060
1970-71	24,996	22,401	17,542	808	65,747
1971-72	24,245	23,583	17,363	1,681	66,872
1972-73	18,623	20,290	14,231	517	53,641
Total boys and girls					
1966-67	115,750	101,779	97,941	3,180	318,689
1967-68	86,733	96,884	92,568	3,766	279,951
1968-69	76,076	95,231	109,808	6,474	287,599
1969-70	89,046	84,536	90,433	5,084	269,099
1970-71	94,793	92,258	75,707	3,243	266,001
1971-72	83,770	96,514	79,910	4,144	264,338
1972-73	62,749	78,945	65,438	1,666	208,798

Derived from: Tableaux de l'Education Nationale.

It may be possible to assemble an adequate picture of the
training options available to young people, but it is extremely difficult to describe the employment options. The distribution of young
people over the wide range of occupational categories is affected by
several variables - age and the level of educational attainment on
the one hand and the sector and nature of the job on the other. Statistics seldom illustrate this relationship. It is possible, however, to show the gap between the level of educational attainment
and that of the jobs actually taken up, especially in the United
States (see Table 15). This helps to explain the disappointment of
young people when expectations - often influenced by parental aspirations - are not realised. It will also be seen that girls tend
to select office jobs while many boys who aspire to white collar jobs
in fact go into production work.

It will also be noticed that the large number of young people
who take unskilled jobs represent a disproportionate percentage of

Table 15

UNITED STATES: FIRST JOBS HELD IN OCTOBER 1971 BY EMPLOYED
1973 SCHOOL DROP-OUTS, HIGH SCHOOL GRADUATES
AND DEGREE RECIPIENTS

(Percentages)

Occupation Groups	Degree Recipients		School Graduates		School Drop-outs	
	Men	Women	Men	Women	Men	Women
Professional and Technical	60.6	64.0	2.2	2.9	–	0.7
Managers and Administrators	3.3	1.3	1.8	0.7	0.8	–
Sales	11.0	3.8	5.8	7.4	5.6	5.0
Clerical and kindred	9.2	22.7	6.4	47.7	4.8	19.3
Service	3.5	6.4	12.0	16.4	10.4	25.0
Craftsmen, Foremen			10.9	–	9.6	–
Operatives	12.5	1.8	32.8	17.1	33.6	24.3
Labourers			22.2	1.9	26.4	2.1
Farm Labourers and Foremen			6.0	1.7	8.8	7.9
Private household	–		–	4.3	–	15.7
Total	100.0	100.0	100.0	100.0	100.0	100.0

Source: B. Reubens, "The Place of the Occupational Component in Education and Training", in Entry of Young People into Working Life – Technical Reports (forthcoming), Tables 4 and 5.

the active work force in such jobs.(1) It is unlikely that this disproportion will be rectified by on-the-job promotion, if only because of the influx of young degree and certificate holders into the labour market. There are accordingly grounds for thinking that many young people who have not had the benefit of sufficient training will have no choice but to accept the least rewarding careers. This fear seems to be justified by the data on wages (see Table 16) and promotion prospects of those who leave school at the compulsory school-leaving age.

3. Factors affecting choices

At least four factors affect the choices of young people as regards the type of training or further study which they would like to pursue or the alternative between education and employment.

i) the structural characteristics of the educational system, notably the sharp distinction between curriculum oriented towards university entrance and curriculum oriented towards work; the discrimination against the latter expressed in selection and elimination;

ii) the unattractiveness of the jobs available, which leads many young people to opt for further study;

iii) the increasing importance of obtaining a degree, which plays a major role in the competition for certain jobs, particularly in the public sector. Many young people, therefore, attach more importance to obtaining a degree than to actually being trained for a specific type of job. This emphasis on obtaining degrees reinforces the selection process within education and the negative effects of meritocracy create an artificial demand for education, thereby keeping at school many reluctant learners who are bored and frustrated and who do not obtain any benefit from continuing study. Indeed, some young people reject technical and vocational training because it is still not always an avenue to higher education at a later stage;

iv) At the same time, there are indications that a number of young people are beginning to view technical and vocational training as a more fruitful option. The current economic

---

1) However, as a result of young people being employed in the less skilled occupations (as unskilled and semi-skilled workers) in France, it is in the industrial sector that the number of under-25-year olds is relatively the highest, representing 21 per cent of the total active population in that sector in 1972. But everything seems to point to the fact that, as they become more educated, young people try to steer clear of these occupations, as the vast majority of former students from every branch of instruction are employed in the public service.

situation and the unfortunate experiences of the older
generations, have contributed to the recent changes in attitude and choice of school subjects.

The attitude of young people towards manual work is of particular interest. It is conditioned not only by the influence of their
education but also by their perceptions of the social structure, the
occupational hierarchy and wage scales. They may also feel that
after completing vocational training they will earn low wages, not
because of a lack of skill but because of their youth and alleged
lack of experience. They may accordingly prefer to do something
other than vocational training in order to earn higher wages during
the early phase of their careers, although their subsequent progress
in some manual trades could have been more advantageous. Young
people may also hesitate to undertake a demanding training for fear
that at the end of the course the skills they acquire will remain
underutilised, whatever the prospects may be in the longer term.

B. THE SEARCH FOR A FIRST JOB

The aim in this section is to describe the channels commonly
used in the transition from school to work. How are young people
distributed among the vast array of occupations? What are the
sources they use to find their first job - personal contacts, career
guidance at school, employment offices or the press and other forms
of advertisement? The answers to these two questions vary considerably depending upon the nature of the relationship between their
school or training institution and the employment sector. This relationship is studied below.

1. Links between school and work

For each individual the links are determined to some extent by
the nature and level of his or her school studies.

   i) Those who have acquired specialised vocational training re-
      lated to job openings experience little difficulty in finding
      a job which corresponds to their abilities. When they do
      have difficulties in finding a job it is usually because em-
      ployers insist upon previous work experience. It should be
      noted that young people with a specialised vocational train-
      ing are often recruited into jobs which at first sight do
      not appear directly relevant to it.
  ii) An effective system is one in which vocational training is
      organised in direct collaboration with industry (for example,
      certain apprenticeship schemes, co-operative education and

sandwich courses) or instruction is given by professional
specialists who devote only part of their time to teaching.
Despite occasional fears that such arrangements may lead to
subservience to the narrow requirements of employers, they
undoubtedly give a useful preparation for work and facilitate placement in a job.

iii) In certain disciplines in higher education, students are in
regular contact with the relevant professional world - for
example, medicine and teaching.

iv) The links between school and work are virtually non-existent
for young people who have not acquired a useable occupational
skill at school. This category includes those who do not go
beyond compulsory schooling, those who drop out of upper
secondary education or complete the upper secondary cycle but
have not followed vocationally oriented courses. It also includes many of those who drop out of higher education and in
many cases those who take liberal arts, social science or
even pure science degrees which do not have a direct corre-
spondence to the needs of industry or the public services.
For all these categories the search for the first job may be
difficult. They may have to take jobs which are far from
corresponding to their qualifications. However, in Europe
those who study at post-secondary level are less likely to
have to accept a low-grade job than in the United States.

This somewhat rudimentary typology of categories of young people
according to the links between their education and the world of work
is obviously affected by a variety of circumstantial factors. Enterprising young people and those with privileged social backgrounds
sometimes succeed in obtaining interesting and well-paid jobs, especially in the tertiary sector. During periods when demand for jobs
exceeds supply it is particularly advantageous to have ready access
to information and good personal contacts - ingenuity in searching
for a job is as important as having qualifications, or even more so.

2. Information

In general, job-information is not well-adapted to individual
needs. It is of little value to young people to know that there are
thousands of jobs to choose from and that in each category of occupation so many people are employed. They cannot relate this type
of statistical information to their own interests. They need some
basic criteria according to which they can assess their own abilities and, in competing for jobs, their hopes of success.

The lack of useable information means that many young people
are led into blind alleys because particular subjects such as biology

or environmental studies tend to become highly fashionable. At the same time they are not necessarily related to realistic occupational outlets. When such outlets do exist, they are often very few and what appears to be a new employment field is in fact a field requiring the application of existing disciplinary qualifications.

Occupational fashions also exist among technicians and scientists. In recent years electronic data processing, operational research and systems analysis have all become popular, but the outlets in these fields have proved to be limited. Paradoxically, in such traditional fields as mechanical engineering, in some countries there is shortage of technicians at every level.

When they are at school young people do not receive a great deal of information about the world of work. The information gathered from older people, especially their parents, has a considerable influence on their choices of career and their attitudes to work. Although by taking temporary or part-time jobs they may be able to form provisional opinions, it is above all when they start searching for their first regular job that they gain real experience of the world of work and some knowledge of how to find jobs. Experience of their first job also has a decisive influence on the choices, attitudes and subsequent careers of young people. For these reasons the information process should be improved. An effort similar to the one in the United States where an occupational Information System is already in operation in nine states would be an important step towards linking education to employment.

3. Placement

Against this background how effective are placement services for young people? In the first place, it should be stressed that placement services are not restricted to dispensing information about job vacancies. They also make use of the training services of the employment authorities. Training programmes are arranged so as to help young people adapt to their first jobs. Mobility grants are given to overcome the unequal distribution of job vacancies. What effects have the placement services had in OECD countries?(1)

    i) Placement services are mostly used by young people with low-level qualifications or with no qualifications at all. That the social services should deal primarily with the underprivileged is an acceptable phenomenon; they should however, help to bring about a real change in their clients' situation.

   ii) Other categories of young people make little use of placement services. In France, for example, a recent survey revealed

---

1) In the United States, approximately 40 per cent of placements by the employment services concern young people under the age of 22.

that only a minority of former students questioned had found
work through such services. They are not really geared to
dealing with young people of high intellectual calibre and
the criteria they apply in matching supply and demand are
not always adapted to actual requirements. Recently, however,
there has been a development of specialised placement services for highly qualified personnel.

iii) Some interesting measures have been adopted to encourage
labour mobility. Many young people cannot find a job near
home because there is no demand for their qualifications in
the areas where they live. Moreover, working conditions and
rates of pay for similar qualifications may vary considerably
from one region to another. However, increased labour mobility cannot provide all the answers to this problem. The areas
with the highest rates of employment and the best jobs are
often in big industrial towns where installation costs and
acclimatisation may pose problems. Labour mobility indeed
has several negative aspects. For example, young people
will often accept jobs in large towns, although the work may
not correspond to their qualifications and young people
without skills who are drawn to the big towns especially from
country areas, fail to find the better jobs for which they
are searching.

4. Unstable employment

The first job a young person obtains does not always offer prospects of further training and promotion. Many young people change
from one job to another, as is particularly the case in the United
States, and this turnover increases the risk of unemployment.

Job changes are an important feature of the process of adapting
to working life and it can be argued that mobility provides young
people with valuable experience and a clearer idea of what they want
to do. This may not always be the case. Although some young people
deliberately leave their jobs because they are not interested in
regular work before military service, for example, others are obliged
to do so because of the terms of their contracts or the unattractive
tasks given to them(1) or their inability to adapt to the world of
work. Many go from one dead-end job to another without acquiring any
training or valuable experience and their attitudes are shaped in a
negative way at a crucial time in their lives.

Many young people with qualifications are obliged to change employment if they wish to climb up the wage scale. This shows to what
extent present employment practices are unfavourable to the employment of young people and the development of skills.

1) Cf. below: Employers' attitudes.

C. SALARIES

It is accepted that the wages of young people who have few or no dependants should remain below the average. What else can be said about young people's wages?

    i) In many countries, as a result of collective bargaining there are graduated wage and salary ranges within each occupational category, based on a starting wage related to initial qualifications. In view of the recent overall increase in income levels it is doubtful whether they offer young people a sufficient incentive to acquire skills, especially in manual crafts where the grading of emoluments flattens out. The graph below gives an example of an agreement which attempts to provide an incentive to acquire additional skills in one sector of French industry. Those who are unable to take advantage of an occupational skill at the outset, despite prolonged school attendance, are in practice excluded from this policy which does not take account of the results obtained through general education.

    ii) Those who leave after compulsory schooling seem to be condemned to the least rewarding careers. In France, a recent survey conducted by the Centre d'Etudes et de Recherches sur les Qualifications has shown that 17-year old wage and salary earners of both sexes who lack a suitable initial vocational training have little chance of escaping from the elementary and even rudimentary tasks in which they are employed. Statistics on wages also show that such young people, whatever their age, find their way up the occupational ladder blocked (see Table 16, first two lines).

    iii) Whereas young people who have proceeded beyond the secondary education stage are concerned mainly about their career prospects, those who have acquired lower level qualifications such as skilled workers and technicians often attach more importance to their starting wage, often because family obligations constrain them to shoulder the burdens of life more quickly and fully - settling into their own accommodation for the first time, helping parents or brothers and sisters, early marriage. It is precisely in the jobs filled by these young people that there are the most striking incongruities.

In all the countries considered it has been found that wage structures do not:

    i) offer promotion and personal development prospects to a critical mass of young people;

France

NATIONAL COLLECTIVE AGREEMENT COVERING THE MAN-MADE AND SYNTHETIC FIBRES INDUSTRY

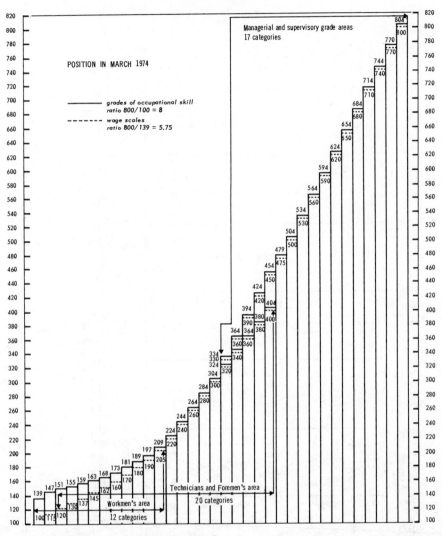

X Axis : Grades of occupational qualification (34 categories).

Y Axis : Skill levels and gross remuneration levels, fringe benefits not included, as compared to the basic standard remuneration, which is periodically established through collective agreement.

NB : 1. Before 1951 those two scales were identical ; the present scale of remuneration is more favourable to the less skilled workers.

2. The minimum wage is fixed by the Government independently of this agreement. It so happens that nobody in this sector would have been paid at this rate. This situation might have been different in other economic sectors, such as the clothing industry.

Table 16

FRANCE: WAGE RATES BY EDUCATIONAL LEVEL IN 1970(1) IN RELATION TO
THE AVERAGE FOR EACH AGE GROUP (= 100)

Educational Level	16-19 years	20-24 years	25-29 years	30-34 years	35-39 years	40-44 years	45-49 years	50-52 years
No diploma	93	91	81	71	72	69	70	71
Certificate of primary education	92	93	90	87	90	86	86	84
First cycle leaving certificate	111	103	107	111	116	130	119	127
Vocational proficiency certificate	120	99	99	101	90	101	104	114
Technician's "baccalauréat"	182	115	125	120	154	147	145	120
Classical or modern baccalauréat Part I	124	108	114	113	137	158	155	166
Classical or modern baccalauréat Part II	140	126	104	133	142	156	179	159
Average wage	100	100	100	100	100	100	100	100

1) Full-time wage earners of both sexes having no secondary activity.

Derived from: R. Pohl and others, Enquête Formation - qualification professionnelle de 1970. Les collections de l'INSEE, Démographie et emploi, No. 32, p. 174.

38

ii) protect young people already employed from having their careers blocked by the entry of graduates straight into higher level posts - this form of blockage is often resented by older workers especially those who have not reached the same level of educational attainment;

iii) nor do they encourage capable young people to acquire occupational skills and generally enhance the prestige of skilled workers in the eyes of the young. Wages and salaries to be offered to these qualified young people could be evaluated on the basis of the cost of the apprenticeship or training to the employer who would otherwise have to train them.

D. ATTITUDES OF YOUNG PEOPLE, SCHOOLS AND EMPLOYERS

When economic constraints are not too stringent the attitudes adopted by young people, teachers and employers become more influential; employment is no longer governed solely by market mechanisms or the intervention of social forces but also by the aspirations and behaviour of individuals. In studying trends in the integration of young people into the world of work it is essential to analyse not only their attitudes but those of educational institutions and employers as well.

1. Young people's attitudes

Young people's attitudes may be defined in relation to education and employment. Can they be categorised in such a way as to indicate in what direction change is desirable?

i) Surveys of young people's aspirations show that they regard education primarily as a means of preparing themselves for a job and for acquiring a higher status in society than their parents. This view of education is usually shared by their parents. It leads young people to embark on long courses of study and to defer the moment when they must choose the job they would like to do.

ii) Clearly, the majority of young people have no fixed occupational goals. Their academic orientation is largely predetermined by factors which are beyond their control or that of their parents. It is therefore not difficult to explain the influence of school values and the consequences of a marking system based on essentially academic criteria, and to recognise that the choice of occupational outlets at secondary education level stems more from rejection or elimination than from a true vocational choice.

iii) School, however, is no longer the sole source of education
or information for the young. They are very conscious of
the discrepancies that can arise between what they are
taught at school and its relevance to their own interests
and the requirements of practical life. Today, more and
more young people are critical of academic studies and there
is a perceptible revival of interest in vocationally oriented
courses, a revival which is undoubtedly connected with the
fear of being unemployed, as are many of those from the immediately preceding generation. Oddly enough, these critical
attitudes affect behaviour in quite different ways; some
young people leave school as soon as possible in order to
take a job; others stay on so as to avoid a transition for
which they feel ill-equipped.

iv) Finally, it is clear that school curricula do not cater ade-
quately for the needs of many young people. Through lack of
interest or the required ability, they derive little or no
benefit from schooling. This has always been particularly
true of the compulsory sector but it is now becoming increasingly true of higher educational levels as well.

All in all, the balance sheet regarding attitudes towards education is somewhat negative in most OECD countries, especially when
it concerns young people from low income families, who are the least
interested by the curricular content and the most motivated by the
acquisition of an occupational skill.

Attitudes towards work may be summed up under five headings:

i) The country surveys show that most young people have a fairly
positive attitude towards work. Whatever their personal wor-
ries about the future, they recognise that the kind of job
that they can do is all-important. The number of those who
reject both society's values and the idea of work remains
relatively few. At the same time, it seems that a negative
attitude to work may be on the increase, particularly among
the more educated.

ii) Whatever their educational level young people are becoming
increasingly reluctant to accept authoritative supervision.
They rebel against a work organisation which imposes constraints and deprives them of initiative and responsibility.
They refuse to accept the same pattern of human relations
which adults have hitherto accepted as an ineluctable social
discipline.

iii) Because they are better educated than older generations they
criticise the boredom of the jobs they are offered and the
difficulty of acquiring professional competence and a rewarding experience.

iv) As far as possible they try to avoid the production line in factories and manual tasks in general. If they have received a general secondary education, they look for office jobs. If they have been to university, they turn to the civil service, teaching or research. Graduates in private firms often want to work in design offices or in research and development rather than production.

v) Young people are often reproached for being less industrious and less willing to shoulder responsibility than their elders. In fact, they are often apathetic in face of working conditions which many adults find equally unbearable. Moreover, they do not acquire appropriate attitudes and work habits at school.

This second balance sheet is more positive in the last analysis. It suggests that the attitudes of young people which are so much criticised are formed by the kind of jobs and salaries offered them and the fact that they feel unable to display their real talents. To some extent the behaviour of young people highlights some of the unattractive features of contemporary working life which adults themselves find less and less acceptable.

2. The teaching profession

The attitudes of teachers have an undoubted influence on the transition problem. Three characteristics of the teaching profession call for comment:

i) Teachers are not sufficiently aware of the preoccupations of industry and commerce. This may be because of their status and their cultural and social characteristics, which in the past, however, gave them a privileged social role.

ii) Some educators distrust the world of work, of enterprises and the very notion of profit.

iii) Teachers as a rule have a tendency to value theory and abstract reasoning more than practical activity.

The teaching profession is therefore inclined to emphasise education as a preparation for roles which are not direcly productive, such as research, teaching, conceptual functions, rather than as an inducement to production and management functions. This ties up with the way employers judge the situation.

3. Employers

Employers' attitudes are determined by their perceptions of the education system and their views about young people in general.

Employers' attitudes to the education system often seem contradictory, especially their attitudes to young people who have completed secondary and university education. On the one hand, they demand increasingly higher educational qualifications, even when these do not reflect useable vocational skills or do not correspond to job requirements. On the other hand, they complain that young people are inadequately prepared for the jobs available to them. This complaint is mainly made about those with post-compulsory/post-secondary education; in France, for instance, complaints centre on those who have had a traditional type of university education.

The attitudes of employers to young people tend to be influenced by their experience of those who left school early with the minimum of education. This is the group which profits least from compulsory schooling in terms of intellectual development, vocational orientation and constructive attitudes. In some countries, they may represent more than 25 per cent of the age group.

Many employers are reluctant to recruit young people into permanent jobs (see Table 17). They consider that young people are not sufficiently motivated before the age of 25 to justify expenditure on training programmes and a guarantee of job security. Some employers also feel that the protection afforded the young in the form, for example, of social security benefits is scarcely likely to stimulate them to make consistent efforts (see Table 18). In certain countries, guarantees of a minimum wage or equal pay for equal work, as given for instance in the Netherlands, may reinforce their reluctance to employ young people.

In many countries young men are conscripted into military service and as a result their induction into working life is interrupted or deferred. The existence of military service, especially when the law requires that those already in a job are entitled to return to that job, inevitably influences employers' hiring policies. Young people attending post-secondary institutions are not usually affected by conscription since they tend to complete their period of military service straight after their studies. However, young people who leave school early have to face the problem of finding a job before their military service. It is this category which employers hesitate to recruit into jobs which belong to a career structure.

Table 17

UNITED STATES: EMPLOYER HIRING PRACTICES TOWARDS YOUNG PEOPLE

Towns	% of establishments not hiring for full-time jobs under 20(1)	
	Office	Non-Office
Atlanta	64	60
Detroit	46	60
Cleveland	45	48
Baltimore	66	70
Milwaukee	51	55
Los Angeles	61	66
Battle Creek	61	76
Auburn	49	65
Galvston	48	55
El Paso	55	63

Jobs	% of employers not wanting to hire persons under 21 for "career" jobs(2)	
	St. Louis	New York City
Bank Teller	90	30
Cashier	94	78
Hotel Clerk	100	80
Shipping & Receiving Clerk	70	19
Arc Welder	90	49
Press Feeder	47	25
Production Machine Operator	82	28
Wire Worker	85	40
Orderly	66	85

Sources: 1) Thomas Gavett, et al. Youth Unemployment and Minimum Wages, Bureau of Labor Statistics, 1970, Chapter IV, pp. 68-77.
2) Daniel Diamond and Hrach Bedrosian, Industry Hiring Requirements and Employment of Disadvantaged Groups, New York University School of Commerce, 1970.

Table 18

FRANCE: TREND OF THE POPULATION AVAILABLE TO SEEK EMPLOYMENT, BY SEX AND BY AGE

Age	June 1968			March 1974			April-May 1975		
	M	F	Tog.	M	F	Tog.	M	F	Tog.
	Percentages								
less 25 years	33.5	43.5	38.8	35.3	45.7	41.1	37.2	44.5	40.8
25-49 years	40.7	38.0	39.5	41.0	38.5	39.6	45.8	42.6	44.2
50 years and over	25.8	18.5	22.5	23.7	15.8	19.3	17.0	12.9	15.0
Total	100.0	100.0	100.0	100.0	100.0	100.0	100.0	100.0	100.0
	Thousands								
	194.6	155.8	350.4	196.3	244.2	440.5	373.4	363.7	737.1

Source: INSEE, Economie et Statistique, décembre 1975.

III. CONCLUSIONS

Until only a few years ago the transition of young people from school to working life was not a major problem for governments. Although the level and type of education and training provided was not always consonant with the needs of the economy, economic expansion was on such a scale that school leavers on the whole had little difficulty in finding a job which seemed appropriate to their educational achievement. By means of apprenticeship, on-the-job experience or additional training, they were able to raise their initial qualifications. For the most gifted and enterprising among them the requirements of an expanding economy opened up promotion and career prospects.

Today the traditional mechanisms for maintaining the input of skills and qualifications required in each occupational sector by recruiting young people no longer seem to work effectively. Despite their generous expenditure on education during recent years, most governments in industrialised countries still have a youth problem and are attempting to find ways to facilitate the entry of young people into working life.

The key features of the present situation reflect both the particular characteristics of the younger generation and those of the world of work:

- there is a gap between the aspirations and expectations of the young and the employment conditions of current production processes;
- there is a discrepancy between the initial education and training received and the actual qualifications required in the various economic sectors as regards knowledge, working habits, attitudes and the capacity to adapt;
- the segmentation of the labour market and the wage and salary structure make it difficult for young people to know what kind of career to pursue;
- there is a divorce between the value system of the industrial society and the ideas of young people which are based on their opinion of society and to some extent on their reluctance to accept its foundations and constraints.

The present investigation of the entry of young people into working life leads to the conclusion that, although the present economic climate is unfavourable, the underlying causes of the problem are primarily of a structural nature. In these circumstances, it is less important to dwell on the relative weight of cyclical or structural factors and imbalances than to identify those policies which are likely to facilitate the entry of the young into working life.

In a society in which it is difficult to guarantee full employment and in which the difficulties of integrating the young into work seem to be greater than ever, public authorities realise that they must do more than simply expand schooling or pay unemployment benefits. Recent policy developments indicate that governments are attempting to ensure that there is better preparation for work within the school system and to provide new training opportunities and effective guidance and placement services, especially for those who would otherwise find themselves at a loss on the labour market. It is however clear that specific measures in favour of young people will not suffice unless they are a part of a co-ordinated policy for creating new jobs and providing wage and salary incentives to those with specific skills and abilities. Such a policy must also ensure that employment structures evolve.

A. EDUCATION

How can every young person be given the right preparation for employment? The recent experiences of countries like France and the United States which have attempted to promote occupational and technical courses alongside academic subjects show that this is no easy task. The pull of cultural traditions is such that those who take these new courses have no guarantee of higher salaries or prospects for a more satisfactory career. As a consequence, the selection process continues to favour the traditional subjects which attract the most fitted or socially privileged. Recent experience shows, however, that an unfavourable employment situation can, with the lapse of time, make young people change their educational choices, as has been seen in Sweden and the United States, and become more conscious of occupational outlets that correspond to the various educational options.

Satisfactory preparation for employment for young people is not merely making a choice between general and vocational education. Just as they are given civics instruction, so they should be informed about the environment of work, social laws, the way in which collective bargaining takes place, the role of the enterprise in economic life and, above all, the importance of economic activity for the

45

well-being of society. Preparation for working life is not simply a question of technical and occupational training.

However, if appropriate instructional techniques are used, is it possible to inculcate qualities and skills with an occupational value through general education? A general education does seem to give suitable qualifications for a certain number of occupations, notably in the service sector but it would be useful to know more about actual competencies required in these occupations, which are often obscured by the technical or organisational aspects of work. This demand is already recognized in several countries. In Denmark, for example, new instructional methods and changing subject matter in higher education reflect that fact that it is questioned not so much for the knowledge content as for the absence of occupational qualities.

Since general education is by no means a suitable preparation for all jobs, it is important to look at the methods of vocational education and training. Opinions differ widely about the contribution of technical and professional training to individual career development and to economic relevance. Thus, in the United States there is no general unanimity on this issue. In Europe, there is a tendency to favour development of this type of education in view of the quality of technical education, the shortage of skilled manpower and, not least, the interests of a large proportion of the school population. At the same time, it does not follow that technical and occupational education should take place within the formal education system.

School is not the only place in which a general education may be acquired. Nor is it the only place to acquire a vocational training. On the contrary, experience shows that in a number of fields which are not amenable to formal academic methods but call for long experience of work the school cannot contribute a great deal. Schools have their limitations in this area and education cannot be considered to bear the entire responsibility for preparing young people for working life.

It must also be emphasized that technical and occupational education is often seen as a dead-end since it does not lead in practice to higher levels of education, particularly not to third level education. Here again, opinions may differ about what policies to adopt. It is generally agreed, however, that occupational upgrading should be made easier by means, for example, of a system of recurrent education.

In general, occupational training suffers from a striking lack of resources, particularly as regards higher level skills both in manual and technical occupations. The funds devoted to it might well be increased in a favourable economic climate. These funds should be no less augmented in a time of economic recession. There is general agreement that everyone should have the opportunity to acquire a marketable skill.

To technical, it is necessary to add social and psychological considerations. Young people now leaving compulsory schooling have a different mentality from their predecessors. They are not disposed to accept dogmatic instruction which to them seems remote from real life. For this reason methods used in the teaching of adults might well be applied to their needs. Such considerations offer a new perspective to the problem of vocational education.

If every young person is to receive adequate preparation for employment, it is evident that major changes are required at the post-compulsory level. The present enquiry has led to the following conclusions.

- The quality of compulsory schooling predetermines in many ways the student's capacity to benefit from subsequent training and to adapt to working life. Far higher priority should be accorded to this level of education where the objective is to give all young people a common educational experience. Yet it is difficult to reconcile this objective with the variety of interests and aptitudes of young people coming from different socio-economic backgrounds, especially as many of them will not continue their studies beyond compulsory schooling. Some form of individualised learning, which could mark a first differentiation would enable some young people to begin their preparation for working life at the secondary level.
- At the post-compulsory level, especially in upper secondary education (in European countries), a more flexible curriculum is desirable. Alongside the general education and traditional methods appropriate for some students there is a need for freer forms of study, such as setting aside periods or blocks of time for part-time employment, social service and cultural, artistic and craft activities.
- In many cases, entirely new options may be necessary to facilitate or ensure satisfactory transition from school to work. These might take the form of part-time education or apprenticeship adapted to the technical and social demands of society.
- Finally, it is essential to strengthen the links between higher education and employment. In Europe at least, a higher education commonly leads to a career in the public services, teaching or research. If it is too soon to speak of the saturation of these three areas of employment, it is nevertheless clear that in the immediate future the possibility of recruitment to them will be limited. This implies that

graduates must be willing to take up non-traditional occupations (as they already do in the United States) or to find a way to acquire a professional qualification.

In conclusion, if the education system cannot be expected to bear the entire responsibility for occupational training, it must nevertheless play an indispensable part in determining the occupational character of the young generation. One of its obvious responsibilities is to assist the young to make adequate preparation for their future careers and ensure that exit levels correspond to entry levels in the occupational structure. This may be achieved either by equipping them with a qualification that is already marketable or with an orientation which lends itself to an apprenticeship, alternating periods of study and work or a work/training contract, that is, arranging for a transitory period between school and full absorption into employment.

B. EMPLOYMENT

The first point to be made is that the organisation and content of work do not as a rule correspond to the expectations of the new work force. Neither the power nor the salary structures nor the distribution of career opportunities seem appropriate to young people. The widening gap between the aspirations of the young and the actual conditions of employment seem to indicate that a transition period between full-time education or training and employment might be helpful. This entails adopting new recruitment and induction policies, providing entry jobs as well as opportunities for further training and adaptation to the world of work.

A second point to be made is that traditional employment policies aimed at improving the functioning of the labour market may not be very efficient as far as young people are concerned. It is true that they help many young people to obtain a job and find their way in the world of work and that they facilitate adjustments between supply and demand. Nevertheless, they serve only a limited category of young people. There is general agreement that further development of public employment services would benefit the young, but in order to bridge the gap between young people's abilities and employment requirements, it is clear that programmes are necessary on a far bigger scale than at present.

It may be argued that young people deserve no more attention than other vulnerable groups of workers. Indeed, this report acknowledges that adult workers with family responsibilities merit preferential treatment. At the same time, if youth employment problems become permanent, specific measures must be considered, since the renewal and vigour of the work force depend on the input of new skills and abilities.

Public policies over the whole economic field affect employment in many ways. Policy measures that affect the distribution of the work force or the combination of production factors exert an influence on youth employment either by their impact on recruitment policies or by the changes in skills requirements which they bring about. Since it is extremely difficult to take account of all these influences in framing overall employment policies direct measures in favour of youth employment can be justified.

Whatever the efforts of the education authorities to provide a vocational preparation for all young people, employment authorities as well as employers clearly have a major responsibility with respect to occupational training. As recent experience shows, employers cannot count on recruiting young people who are already suitably trained. It is therefore in their own interests to offer young people more training opportunities than at present. However, so as to ensure that young people retain a certain freedom of choice and acquire qualifications which they can use in other jobs, it seems appropriate for governments to assume ultimate responsibility for this training and to contribute to its costs. Finally, it is to the advantage of employers to adapt their employment structures and recruitment policies to provide more opportunities for part-time or temporary jobs and to create "entry" jobs that offer work experience of longer-term value to the young recruits.

There is ample evidence that structures designed to provide a transition period between school and full-time work for those who lack occupational skills will be effective in the medium term. Such a transition may be considered from several points of view:

- First, the responsibility of the public authorities is no
  longer restricted to that of the Education Department or to
  distributing unemployment benefits. Recent policy developments show that it extends to the interlude between leaving
  school and settling into a stable job, firstly by providing
  really efficient educational and vocational guidance and
  placement services. Such services are specially needed in
  countries where young people experience difficulty in finding
  a job before entering compulsory military service;
- Second, it is important that, within employment, young people
  should have the opportunity during an initiation period to
  acquire such experience and qualifications as they may lack.
  In this connection recent experiments in Yugoslavia and France
  are worth noting;

- Third, specific programmes are being designed to provide
  occupations for young people during this transition period
  either within firms or through job-creation programmes. Such
  programmes aim as far as possible at providing jobs in the
  regular work environment, together with relevant training
  opportunities. These schemes have many features in common
  with apprenticeships, although they may apply to other than
  traditional apprenticeship skills.

This latter idea, which aims at increasing the number of options
offered to the young, entails a particular effort by employers and
closer collaboration between them and the education authorities. As
compared with more traditional manpower training courses, with limited
ambitions, such schemes may provide opportunities for bridging the
structural gap between young people's abilities and employment requirements.

Another conclusion relates to financial awards for occupational
skills. The present salary structure dates from a past in which
educational benefits were unevenly distributed with the result that
today school-leavers who possess medium-level skills find themselves
penalised. It would seem essential to review salary scales with
the object of ensuring that young people will receive wages commen-
surate with the effort they have made to acquire an occupational
skill. A carefully designed incentive scheme would encourage suitable
candidates to take up technical occupations.

However, this proposal, as with all proposals regarding wage
structures, raises a delicate and complex problem. Furthermore, in
countries where efforts are under way to narrow wage differentials
(as in Sweden) or to upgrade manual work (as in France) - both
policies tending to raise the base of the wage structure - there is
a risk that certain skills, already insufficiently rewarded, will be
penalised, and that in the long run the economy will be deprived of
vital skills. In the United States it would seem that wage differentials are not a major issue. However, in those countries where the
hierarchy of occupations and wages is still related significantly to
educational attainment rather than actual skills, collective bargaining agreements could lead to better rewards for acquired skills.
This is an area in which detailed study is called for not only in
relation to the young but to the entire labour force.

This proposal also aims at restoring, or at least promoting,
some coherence in the evaluation of degrees and diplomas at the
moment of recruitment. In many countries, the expansion of education
combined with competition for jobs has led to undue importance being
attached to higher educational qualifications, especially in the
public sector. It is now essential to take account of individual

aptitudes and skills as well as scholastic attainments. The present
situation leads to criticism of the meritocratic principle; criticism
that is justified when high salaries are linked to educational qualifications rather than occupationally valid ones. To relate salaries
to actual skills is all the more necessary if the objective of
equality of opportunity is to be pursued, especially for those adults
for whom there was no scope for further study when they were young.

C. GUIDANCE

In OECD countries it is politically out of the question to
direct young people into particular courses of study or for education
to be subordinated to the exigencies of the labour market. At present, there are considerable differences of opinion about the prin-
ciples on which guidance should be based. However, three points of
agreement may be noted:

a) it is desirable to identify and encourage individual aspirations and aptitudes whether they are related to occupations
   or not;
b) a guidance service must respect freedom of choice and offer
   more reliable information about employment prospects;
c) it is necessary to establish conditions of employment which
   permit greater freedom and more opportunities for personal
   development. How can these requirements be met?

First, in many countries young people tend to be distributed
among various branches of study by means of a more or less rigorous
selection process. This is contrary to the objective of allowing all
individuals to develop their capacities to the fullest possible extent. Orientation presupposes that students are genuinely free to
keep their options open, but this point is already controversial.
Certain critics feel that the diversification of education leads to
social selection and that in the interests of equality of opportunity
everyone should share the same educational experience, especially
during the period of compulsory schooling. It has been noted, however, that this policy may increase the handicap of those young
people who are least able to master abstract subjects or who belong
to underprivileged social groups.

Nor is there agreement over the priorities to be observed in
improving guidance services. Whereas some people believe that the
most gifted students should be specially encouraged, others argue in
favour of giving priority to compensatory education for the less
gifted. The debate continues. However, by examining the conditions
of integration into working life and society's need for highly qualified personnel, it should be possible to work out a reasonable compromise.

Secondly, guidance services should, ideally, take into account employment needs and possibilities in the short, medium and long term. Experience shows that this is hard to achieve. Moreover, it would be misguided to base vocational guidance on an extrapolation of prevailing occupational structures. No doubt, quantitative projections can be a useful guide to educational planning, notably by highlighting the labour market's limited absorptive capacity. It is however more important to specify the nature and variety of qualifications that are required. This implies that planning should be confined to laying down general guidelines for educational development while the development of skills in accordance with personal abilities and interests should be encouraged. In practice, the advent on the labour market of more highly educated and qualified people is likely to result in changes in employment structures. As the average level of education rises, the gap between young people's educational attainments narrows and "qualitative" guidance assumes increasing importance. Moreover, choices are no longer dictated by a desire to reach the highest university levels, as recent experience shows.

Thirdly, vocational guidance should enable young people to make rational choices. At present choices are determined by educational structures as well as by students' perception of occupational hierarchies and working conditions, and to some extent by cyclical fluctuations in employment.

In the course of their education, young people are constantly influenced by these factors. The task of vocational guidance is to help them. In order to do this

i) students must be given information about available education and training options and categories of occupation. At present this information is by no means adequate. Further research is undoubtedly required if young people are to be given a faithful and useable account of the opportunities available to them. In this connection, it is expected that valuable results will come from the Occupational Information Systems Grants Programme currently being tried out in nine States by the United States Department of Labor. The collection of social statistics and systematic analysis of the nature and content of jobs and occupational careers are essential elements in such research;

ii) students must be helped to develop skills in decision-making, to know how to assess their own potential and think for themselves. This should be a permanent objective throughout their studies and may indeed be considered an essential part of their preparation for future economic and social life;

iii) guidance should not be given exclusively at terminal stages
such as the end of compulsory schooling or the entry point
into higher education. Rather it should be available from
the beginning of compulsory schooling right up to the time
when a young person settles into an established job;

iv) educational and vocational guidance should include detailed
and continuing monitoring of changes in educational and employment patterns. It requires planning not in quantitative
terms but in terms of the criteria indicated earlier in this
report. It requires forecasts of the qualities that will
characterise working life in the future rather than the
specification of recruitment quotas.

Close co-ordination between school and out-of-school guidance
and placement services is essential. Although it may not be felt
appropriate to group them into a single service, there must at least
be more integration at regional and local levels.

D. SPECIAL PROGRAMMES FOR YOUTH

Since it has not been possible to provide adequate guidance for
young people nor to give all of them appropriate occupational training, nor to resolve their employment problems by traditional policies,
a number of special programmes which provide job opportunities for
young people have been introduced in many countries.

Many of these programmes involve social or community services.
In practice, however, their effects have not always been clearly defined. It is therefore useful to define better the nature, the form
and the objectives of these programmes.

i) It does not seem politically feasible for OECD Member countries
to replace or supplement compulsory military service by some
other form of compulsory service. Discussions on this possibility within the International Labour Organisation suggest
that such service might be construed as forced labour. The
underlying principle, however, appears to be accepted in
some of the less well developed countries.

ii) Certain kinds of programmes, on the basis of voluntary and
short-term participation, can provide young people with a
useful activity and some practical training in such areas as
environmental control, social work, archaeological excavation
and service in developing countries. In Portugal, for example, a year's "civic service" has been instituted for those
wishing to undertake study at university level.

iii) Another development is the creation or deliberate encouragement by the public authorities of permanent employment sectors designed to satisfy new public needs or to foster certain
types of qualifications which the economic system does not at
present encourage. The financing of these sectors may be
taken over subsequently by the appropriate authorities or
even by private industry and commerce.

iv) Finally, there are programmes expressly catering for unemployed young people, usually formulated in the light of the
prevailing economic situation and aimed at preparing the
participants for their further employment. As a consequence
they focus on more traditional skills and activities.

These four examples illustrate what may be done to help young
people in economies where the overall workload is diminishing, adult
employment is protected and the problem of youth employment may be
due more to long-term than to circumstantial factors.

It should be noted that young people may participate in job
creation programmes designed for adults. In that case it is more
accurate to refer to programmes from which the young may benefit
along with all other workers. At the same time, their participation
in such programmes may be disproportionately larger than that of
other groups. It is also to be noted that if these programmes are
to be viable, they require the presence of some qualified people who
are not necessarily unable to find employment.

A more thorough examination of each programme is required. The
present proposals have not answered the following questions:

i) what are the entry qualifications required for every type of
employment?

ii) are these programmes only a means of providing the public
sector with cheap labour?

iii) are these programmes in competition with private firms or
other public sectors?

iv) how do these programmes facilitate eventual placement in
regular employment?

With regard to these questions, it would be interesting to
analyse the experiences of Canada (Opportunities for Youth, Avenir
Jeunesse, Local Initiative Programmes) and Europe (Youth Enterprise
in the United Kingdom, the Mondragon project in Spain). Such an
analysis would show whether or not the young people (or older
workers) attracted to these programmes have subsequently found jobs
and in what ways some of these programmes might become permanently
established and self-supporting. Recent experience shows that relatively small financial outlays have enabled young people to undertake
activities of value to the community which are not as a rule a part

of the existing public services. These programmes are useful, therefore, from two points of view: they offer employment to young people of a type that they would not otherwise find within the established framework of the public services or the open labour market and that enables them to perform a valuable service to the community.

A fundamental question is to identify in what sectors of the economy such programmes can be launched and at what levels they can be managed. Many argue in favour of social services. Is this a realistic orientation and is it likely to appeal to the young? If social service programmes are to reach a sizeable dimension they must presumably be conceived in terms of job creation within the larger context of a policy for employment. It is generally acknowledged today that it is preferable to create or maintain jobs rather than pay unemployment benefits.

Finally, there is the question of the financing of such programmes, which is usually presented as an alternative to paying unemployment benefits or educational charges. However, financing must make allowances for the costs of complementary training, equipment and management. It is obvious that, despite political pressure to respond to unemployment and the dissatisfaction of young people, priorities should be set in terms of the efficiency and ultimate social value of these programmes.

Part II

CURRENT RESPONSES
TO
YOUTH UNEMPLOYMENT

INTRODUCTION

More than at any time since the end of World War II, OECD countries that have been affected by recession since 1974 have shown
concern about youth unemployment. The latter half of 1975 and 1976
posed a particular challenge to public policy because the new entrants to the labour force from schools and universities flooded the
market at a time when total unemployment was high and, in some countries, continued to rise. In some countries (e.g. Germany) rising
youth unemployment is a distinct departure from the previously favoured position of young workers in the labour market; in others the
conjunctural* developments have exacerbated a deteriorating situation
for youth which began in the mid-1960's in, for instance, the United
Kingdom, Sweden, Australia, France and Belgium, and even longer ago
and more seriously in the United States.

---

* "Conjunctural" is used interchangeably with "cyclical".

I. YOUTH UNEMPLOYMENT IN RECESSION

Recession means that more people in the labour force experience one or more spells of unemployment and that the duration of each spell is longer on the average. Many countries have found that young people are particularly vulnerable in economic downturns. Employers facing a reduction in activity do not hire new entrants as freely as before; and, if reductions in force are required, the most recently hired, usually young workers, are the first to be dismissed. Collective bargaining agreements, legislation and social policy sanction such procedures.

A. MEASURING UNDERUTILISATION OF YOUTH

The initial impact of the current recession fell heavily on youth in a large number of countries. From late 1973 to late 1974 in the nine EEC countries, youth unemployment (under 25) rose by 49 per cent while the increase for all ages was 32 per cent. Some countries showed even sharper differences: in Denmark, for example, young people under 25 had a 405 per cent increase in unemployment over the year, while total unemployment rose by 335 per cent. Belgium's general rate of increase was 33 per cent, but youth registered a 64 per cent jump.[1] Not all countries show this pattern, of course. In Japan where new entrants are especially favoured, the brunt of such unemployment as occurred has been borne by older workers; as late as 1975, the employment service reported seven vacancies for each junior high school graduate and four for each senior high school graduate. In the United States teenage unemployment rates did not rise as rapidly as adult ones, so that the ratio of teenage to adult unemployment rates actually declined in the initial phases of the recession.

As the recession wore on and unemployment continued to rise, the youth share in several countries rose more slowly than the adult. In Denmark, from late 1974 to late 1975, youth unemployment rose by 53 per cent, and the unemployment of persons aged 25 and above rose by 71 per cent. The tendency of the youth share of unemployment to

---

* Reference numbers relate to the list at the end of this report.

fall even as the total number of young unemployed grows is illustrated for France in Table 18, Part I. In the recovery period when
unemployment begins to fall, in some countries young people are
absorbed into employment more rapidly than older workers, but in
others, like the United States, the reverse is true with respect to
teenagers. Many countries now report that young people, especially
teenagers, are left in a relatively more disadvantaged position at
the end of a recession than they were before it began.

The percentage increase in unemployment is only one measure of
the impact of recession. In several countries, namely the United
States, Canada, Italy, the absolute unemployment rates also draw attention to the adverse position of young people. Starting with the
very high unemployment rate of 14.5 per cent in 1973, American teenagers had a 20.3 per cent unemployment rate in May 1975 and black
teenagers moved from an official rate of 30.3 per cent in 1973 to a
1975 recession high of 40.2 per cent. These teenage rate increases,
while smaller proportionately than those of the American 20-24 year
group or the whole labour force, are sufficient to establish a serious
recession problem among young people.

International comparisons of unemployment rates are difficult.
In some countries, e.g. the United States, Canada, Japan and Sweden,
unemployment rates are drawn from labour force surveys; in others,
such as the United Kingdom, France, Belgium, the Netherlands, they
are based on registrations; in others, e.g. Denmark, they are derived
from both. Some include full time students seeking part-time or
seasonal employment (United States); others do not. This paper,
however, does not attempt to provide comparable figures on unemployment, a subject which is being studied by the OECD working party on
employment and unemployment statistics.

As the unemployment rate rises in recession the average duration
of each spell of unemployment also lengthens, but at a somewhat slower
pace. In most countries young workers who lose or leave their jobs
tend always to have shorter spells of unemployment than other age
groups; they appear as a dynamic portion of the labour force, with
volatile participation rates. Although there is an increase during
a recession of the proportion of the young unemployed who become
long-term unemployed, young people on the whole tend to move in and
out of jobs. This is particularly true if new entrants to the labour
market are treated separately. In periods of recession, the time
taken to find a job is perceptibly longer than in more prosperous
periods, but differences between countries are considerable on this
point.

Overt unemployment is not the only evidence to be weighed. The
discouraged or hidden unemployed, those who have given up the search
for work because they believe no suitable jobs are available, are

officially counted in a few countries only. In Sweden, as the number of latent unemployed rises in recession periods, the youth component of this group increases disproportionately.[3]

The recession also causes lower labour force participation rates (the proportion of an age group which is in the labour force) for potential new entrants to the labour market as well as withdrawals from the labour force by discouraged young workers who may have experienced unemployment. Females are particularly likely to show this reaction. Such responses to the decline in economic activity since 1974 have kept the Japanese unemployment rate from rising as much as it might have done otherwise.[4] A special case of withdrawal from the labour force, which also reduces the registered unemployment rates in Western European countries, is the return home of foreign workers, a large proportion of whom are 20 to 30 years old. Reductions in labour force participation rates due to recession constitute hidden unemployment. Withdrawal of young people from the labour force must therefore be considered along with unemployment rates.

In connection with reductions in labour force participation rates, the question arises as to the activities of young people who, in a more favourable economic climate, would have entered or remained in the labour market. A voluntary extension of education has been a frequent response, according to earlier American research.[5] Evidence for many countries in the present recession, such as the United States, the United Kingdom, Australia, Canada and Italy, indicates that education or occupational training still absorb some who might otherwise be unemployed.

Another dimension of youth unemployment in recession is the involuntary reduction of working hours in many countries. Japan has resorted to this alternative to unemployment on a large scale in an effort to protect its system of lifetime employment. Unemployment rates do not take direct account of this aspect of recession, although separate tabulations are made in some countries. In the United States young workers usually bear a disproportionate share of this form of unemployment.

Some analysts would add another effect of recession on youth - the acceptance of lower level and lower paid jobs than might be obtained in times of vigorous economic growth, or taking jobs at substandard wages. It remains to be seen whether the jobs which disappear in a recession are to a large extent those which offer young people an opportunity for advancement and security. If this is the case, recession would mean not only fewer jobs for young people but relatively fewer good jobs.

In calculating the effects of a cyclical downturn on youth employment, all of the factors mentioned above should be taken into account. In international comparisons in particular the amount or rate of registered youth unemployment, even when adjusted for national variations in methods of measurement, is an inadequate yardstick. Because countries differ markedly in the number of discouraged young people in relation to the number who are actually unemployed, a broader view of unemployment must be taken. The effects of decreased job opportunities on labour force participation rates, the resort to less than full-time work or job-sharing, the changes in the composition of jobs for young people, and their willingness to accept lower level jobs as an alternative to unemployment must be taken into account. Some American analysts have devised several experimental subemployment indices that combine the various elements of unemployment rates, duration of unemployment, hidden unemployment, reduced labour force participation rates, hidden part-time work, and substandard wages or earnings. One of the disputed issues is the definition of substandard wages - whether to adopt a single standard or different standards relating to age, family size, and other criteria of need.[6] The subemployment approach to the measurement of youth unemployment is of course valid for other age groups and for periods other than recessions.

In a few European countries there is a disturbing trend which echoes an earlier finding for the United States. It appears that after each recovery from a cyclical downturn since the mid-1960's, the youth share of unemployment has settled at a somewhat higher level than in the previous recovery.[7] Since the time period involved is quite short and the data are not entirely satisfactory in some countries, this reported development requires further investigation in the coming years to see whether the American experience is in fact repeated. United States records show that in 1948 a 3.8 per cent unemployment rate for all ages occurred with a teenage rate of 9.2 per cent and that a 5.6 per cent total rate in 1954 was accompanied by a 12.6 per cent youth rate. But when these total rates appeared again in the 1960's, the corresponding teenage rates were two per cent higher than they had been in the first post-war years. By the 1970's, a 5.6 per cent total rate was accompanied by teenage rates of 16 per cent or more, about 4 per cent above the 1954 level. The rise in teenage unemployment rates, exceeding the rise in the age group's share of the labour force, would be even more marked if total unemployment rates were adjusted for changes in the composition of the labour force or labour force participation rates.[8] If this same trend is established in European countries, it will not be possible to assume that an economic recovery will restore the status quo ante for youth. It may mean that youth unemployment which develops during recessions is perpetuated and reinforced by structural trends.

Some analysts consider that the economy's loss from recession unemployment can be measured by a single figure - the man-hours not worked against the potential man-hours available. An American calculation along these lines raises the official unemployment rate for 1974 of 5.6 per cent to 7.8 per cent.[9] It is possible to refine the calculation further by taking account of the quality of the man-hours not worked as well as the number of man-hours worked below the ability of workers.

B. FALSE UNEMPLOYMENT

It is possible that youth unemployment may be overstated as well as undercounted. One disputed practice, chiefly in the United States, is the inclusion of full-time pupils and students as unemployed when they are unable to find part-time work during the school year. Some are seeking only a few hours work a week, such as baby-sitting or delivery work, but they count as heavily in the unemployment statistics as those who have left school some time ago and who are searching for full-time jobs. The total number of American teenagers unemployed in 1974 would be reduced by almost half if the in-school unemployed were excluded. In the past similar practices have, to a more limited extent, caused the unemployed school leaver figures for the United Kingdom to be overstated. Recently, guidance to Careers Offices has been strengthened to ensure that young people leaving full-time education with a known intention of going on to further education are not classified as school leavers but treated as being in the same category as further education students registered for vacational work. In Italy, it is said, the stated unemployment rates must be adjusted for "black work", jobs which are arranged without payment of the various payroll taxes levied against employers and, sometimes, workers.

Another category counted as unemployed, but disputed, is the young person whose unemployment registration is intended to qualify for social benefits rather than to find work. This **particularly** affects countries which compute unemployment from registrations, pay benefits to young people who have never worked, or require registration as unemployed as a prerequisite for the receipt of other social benefits. The size of the population which takes advantage of such administrative requirements without intending to work is not known, but it is likely that during a recession they are a smaller proportion of all unemployed youth than at other times. Not only are there more genuinely unemployed young people in recession periods, but neither are there jobs available for some who may be indifferent to work, and this provides them with a legitimate place among the unemployed at such times.

The same point can be made about other young people whose attitudes, expectations or requirements cause employers and employment service personnel to declare that they are not seriously interested in working. Yet such charges are made most frequently at times when layoffs and dismissals account for a rising share of idleness, when voluntary job-leaving diminishes, and when the number of vacancies drops. One reason for these charges may be that employers are encouraged by adverse economic conditions and loose labour markets to raise their hiring standards. Some young people resist a downgrading from their previous jobs, or from their hopes if they are new entrants, because they fear the effects on their long-term prospects and their chances of obtaining the type of work and earnings possible under tighter labour markets. Young people also may protect themselves against rejection by employers by adopting attitudes of negligence or hostility toward work. Some of these attitudes are seen in depressed areas or among minority youth even in times of general full employment. Not unexpectedly, the number affected and the intensity of the reaction may rise in a recession.

It may be true that a certain number of cyclically unemployed youth do not really want to work and the external causes, such as the nature of the jobs available to some young people and the values and aspirations imparted by the educational system should be taken into account. The entire burden should not be placed on the attitudes and behaviour of young people. In any case, public policy would be misguided if it discounted large numbers of young unemployed in recession periods as voluntarily idle. On the other hand, however, it is not necessary to accept every last young person in the unemployment statistics as a legitimate candidate for the short-term measures which deal with recession unemployment.

C. EFFECTS ON SUBGROUPS OF YOUTH

Policies launched during recessions to aid unemployed youth must approach the subject in a disaggregated fashion, paying attention to the experience of various subgroups of the youth population during the cyclical downturns. Several categories of youth are commonly designated and divisions are made according to age, sex, educational achievement or level, new entrant status, amount and type of occupational training; minority or disadvantaged status; and area of residence. Studies of this matter reveal that the handicaps of certain subgroups are intensified by recession. Recent French and German inquiries indicate that this is the case in regional and local disparities in youth unemployment.

Sex differences in youth unemployment vary from country to country. For example, EEC data for Member countries from 1966 to 1974 show that male youth unemployment consistently exceeded female in Italy, the Netherlands and the United Kingdom, while the reverse was true in France, Belgium and Germany. In Denmark, Ireland and Luxembourg the differences were small. No distinct effects on the relative position of the two sexes can be discerned in recession years, either within individual countries or more widely across national borders.[12] In examining the impact of cyclical unemployment on the two sexes, account should be taken in most countries of the higher propensity of young women to withdraw from the labour force, and of the national or regional industrial structure.

In times of full employment less attention is paid to the position of disadvantaged young people than in a recession or in situations where youth unemployment is persistent. Adverse conditions stimulate inquiries into the disproportionate amount of unemployment suffered at all times by minority youth, immigrants, the physically, mentally and socially handicapped, and those who leave school without passing examinations or obtaining diplomas. These groups may, in fact, bear a heavier share of total youth unemployment when economic activity is vigorous than when it slows down. But during recession many are identified as disadvantaged who escape notice in better times because they are in employment, however unsatisfactory. Cyclical and structural factors are closely intertwined in the case of these young people and short-term and longer-term public policy necessarily overlap.

When labour force surveys are used to compute unemployment rates by age groups they frequently show that teenagers have higher unemployment rates than young adults. Differences are usually more pronounced for males than females. It can be argued that age as such is not as important an explanation of variations in youth unemployment rates as are several related factors: activity rate of new entrants in the age group, the level of education achieved, and the amount of previous vocational training. Therefore, differential unemployment rates relating to these factors may well be more revealing about the subdivisions within the youth group than mere age. Perhaps the most important factor is indistinguishable from age: experience and the maturity which it brings; an indication of the importance of responsibility is the differential in unemployment rates between all young people and young people who are household heads. This difference was 6 percentage points in the United States in 1974 and 1975.

New entrants to the labour market are considered to be among those most harmed by recession; yet relatively little is known about how they fare in comparison with other young workers, especially because countries vary in their attitudes towards them. The United Kingdom, Germany, Switzerland, Japan and the Netherlands have been consistently more receptive to young new entrants than France, Belgium, Italy, Ireland, the United States, or Canada. There is scattered evidence that in the former group of countries teenage new entrants usually have lower unemployment rates than young workers of the same age, particularly when a high proportion of school leavers have arranged for their jobs before leaving school, as is notably the case in Japan and the United Kingdom. New entrants in the United Kingdom and the Netherlands may be at an advantage over young workers of the same educational attainment who have changed jobs frequently or who are close to the age when adult wage rates must be paid (23 in the Netherlands). The more rapid absorption of 1974 new entrants in the United Kingdom as compared with France was probably partly due to the residual effect of the raising of the school leaving age in 1973 which caused a shortfall in school leavers seeking employment.[13]

New entrants' unemployment can also be analysed with respect to the level of education attained. Do university graduates take less time to find their first jobs than school-leavers from compulsory school and what is the effect of recession on each group? An official British measurement of the unemployment rates of new school-leavers and graduates six months after leaving university uses different statistical sources for each group, and thus it is difficult to make the case for university graduates having the higher entry unemployment.[14] Comparisons using consistent data from the same survey are rare and tend to show that the duration of entry unemployment should be modified by consideration of the type of employment sought. The younger, and less well educated are not only less selective about the jobs they accept, but are also more prepared to take temporary employment while waiting for something better to come along.

It is more difficult to measure unemployment rates for young workers in relation to educational level because the teenage work force by its very nature has few or no university graduates and has fewer years of education, lower levels of skill, and less work experience on average than young adults. One satisfactory procedure could be to examine, not the whole labour force but an age group in which it can be assumed that the vast majority of members have completed whatever formal education they are likely to obtain; for most countries, the best choices would be the ages of 20-24, although it can be argued that this would not give an accurate picture of some young people's experience when they first enter the labour market. Countries that have published useable data almost always have found consistently lower unemployment rates associated with higher levels of education, although the margins have been narrowing as average educational levels have risen.[15] Although no firm conclusion can be drawn from the statistical data available, evidence suggests that in some countries young graduates tend to find themselves in situations very similar to those of young people with lower levels of education. Still to be determined are the effects of recession on the relative unemployment rates and other aspects of underutilisation of both new entrants and young workers classed in accordance with the various educational levels they have reached.

New entrants leaving at a given level of education may also differ in the time taken to find a first job because of differences in the content of their education. It can be reasonably supposed that those whose education included specific vocational subjects will find first jobs more quickly or will find better jobs than those who completed the same number of years but in general education. Few countries can conduct such an inquiry at the compulsory school level because occupational skills are rarely imparted there and studies are invalid if they compare 15 or 16 year-old entrants with 18 year-old entrants who have completed a few years of occupational preparation at school. In many countries too, the structure of upper secondary education does not permit such investigations because general education predominates, and it is assumed that occupational skills will be imparted after starting work, and that employers do not wish young entrants to have prior training. In Sweden's upper secondary school, a short occupational component is built in for each pupil so, here again, no comparisons can be made. In the first part of this report, it has been emphasized that, in addition to age and educational level, the possession of occupational skills or qualifications is an increasingly important factor in the access to jobs. The situation varies from country to country according to the requirements of the labour market and the availability of people with specific skills. In countries such as France or Sweden, young people with specific qualifications, whatever the educational level, have little difficulty in finding jobs; those from general education or with little vocational preparation experience a high risk of unemployment. Countries also differ greatly in their capacity and willingness to absorb secondary school graduates with occupational preparation at a suitable level of employment. Shortcomings in this respect undoubtedly explain part of the failure of American high school graduates with vocational courses to show better labour market achievements than those with academic courses.[16]

When all young workers and not just new entrants are considered it is necessary to take account of formal and informal on-the-job training which, in many countries, is more important than prior occupational preparation. Unemployment rates are lower and future

68

prospects are brighter for those whose work experience has included opportunities for training. However, training is not a protection against recession; a recession does bring unemployment to trained young workers, often a relatively greater amount than to the untrained whose normal share of unemployment is very disproportionate to their numbers.[17]

For those who have had post-secondary education, the unemployment rates and types of job obtained differ as between those who have specific occupational preparation and those who do not. Many of the courses with occupational content have fewer registrations than are justified by labour market demand and the graduates consequently obtain jobs fairly easily. But a more important reason for this is the deliberate limitation on enrolments applied to courses with specific occupational content. In effect, the courses with numerus clausus provide the labour market with particular skills and thus facilitate the entry of graduates into employment or self-employment. Some of these courses are even responsive to cyclical and structural changes in the demand for their graduates, as is the case with teacher training in a number of countries. If unlimited entry were available to all post-secondary courses that prepare for specific occupations, the situation of these favoured students might well be adversely affected.

However, so long as the majority of students continue to choose the liberal and fine arts, foreign languages and other subjects that are difficult to relate to occupations, they are likely to have a less satisfactory initial employment experience than those who prepare for specific occupations. In recession, those with post-secondary education, whether specific or not, either have increasing difficulty in finding employment or accept lower positions than they believe their qualifications deserve. A combination of both solutions is most likely in countries where post-secondary and especially university graduates are widely employed outside teaching and the public services and where social status considerations do not deter employers and job-seekers from considering non-traditional jobs.

II. SHORT-TERM MEASURES TO COMBAT YOUTH UNEMPLOYMENT

A. HOW MUCH PRIORITY FOR YOUTH?

Unemployment is regarded as harmful whatever the age of its victims. Is there then any reason to treat youth unemployment as more serious than that of other age groups? In fact, many hold that the unemployed family head should be the focus of social and government policy; an economic advisor to the French President recently asserted this principle.[18] On the other hand, there are arguments for making youth a high priority group. Discouragement and disappointment at the outset of working life are said to leave permanent scars as well as depriving a young person of the chance to acquire good work habits and attitudes. The alternatives to which unemployed young people may turn also cause concern. In American cities rising youth unemployment is associated with increased crime, violence, suicides, drug addiction, and prostitution. European countries, already wary of discontented and radicalized students, have had youth demonstrations over unemployment and are sensitive to the political implications of mounting youth unemployment.[19] It has been emphasized in the first part of this report that the occupational integration of young people is central to the renewal of the work force, and that it is this which makes it possible to prepare society's future development. Even without a definite decision to give youth the highest priority in anti-recession measures, a clear case can be made for special attention.

The fact that young people suffer disproportionately from unemployment during periods of recession does not automatically indicate that programmes should be designed exclusively for them or that a policy for young people should be launched in isolation from general programmes to combat cyclical unemployment. Some separate programmes may indeed be required, particularly for new entrants whose needs may not be identical with those of young people who have worked. But all special programmes are best developed by the staff which is also concerned with devising the programmes for other age groups. It is necessary also to weigh the benefits of a special emphasis on youth against the costs of reinforcing an isolation from adult life and the work world which many young people already feel.

The actual programmes instituted in the various countries during recession periods are usually related to the existing programmes. In fact, some countries rely chiefly on an expansion of existing programmes, some of which may have been initiated in the previous recession period. Operative programmes may be modified to fit the needs of a particular age group or other category. This procedure works well in countries such as Sweden where a minimum amount of legislation and financial negotiation is needed to expand programmes, where a wide variety of manpower measures are operative at all times, and plans are made ahead of time for the contingency of an increase in unemployment. Other countries must initiate complicated legislative sessions before new programmes can be launched or old ones extended, thus losing valuable time or ending up with unbalanced or excessively restricted programmes. Because of differences in traditions, styles of operation, values and basic institutions among the OECD countries, there is considerable variation in the degree of continuity in programmes, the speed of response in a recession, the mix of measures adopted, and the amount of commitment to a programme to combat unemployment.

To cope with the unemployment of young people, it is essential for a set of selective and differentiated programmes to be developed. The first part of this report has illustrated the diversity of situations in which young people find themselves; from this it follows that individual measures should be examined in the light of their relative efficiency in coping with the various categories of young people.

The choice of such measures should be based on a number of criteria. It is important, for example, to avoid subsidising unproductive or inflationary solutions; one must be wary, too, of measures that would increase the segregation of young people implicit in occupational programmes devised exclusively for them. In the same context, measures that favour youth but are harmful to other categories should be avoided. On the positive side, programmes should aim to help through the existing training system because, in many cases, the number of trainee places (apprenticeships, for example) tend to be reduced in times of economic recession. Particular attention should be given to less privileged youth. All such programmes should take account of longer term trends and overall industrial policy by encouraging those types of training which have been identified as insufficiently developed within the system.

It may be difficult to devise policies that respond to all of these concerns. However, such criteria should be given proper weight and attention when specific programmes are looked at in the broader context of national situations and general employment policies.

B. POTENTIAL EFFECTS ON YOUTH OF MEASURES
AGAINST GENERAL UNEMPLOYMENT

Four main types of action which have a potential effect on
youth unemployment may be distinguished:

a) general measures to stimulate the whole economy or specific
   regions or industries; e.g., monetary and fiscal actions,
   the Swedish investment reserve system, regional development
   grants and loans. The major constraints arise from fears of
   stimulating inflationary forces.

b) measures to maintain employment or counter unemployment without specification of particular age groups. As these programmes work out, they may become mainly youth programmes,
   or youth may be relatively neglected or even harmed.

c) reduction of the labour force through early retirement, lower-
   ing pensionable age, etc.

d) work-sharing or short-time work, with compensation for
   partial unemployment.

Such measures have already been discussed in the context of
general employment policies.* As far as young people are concerned,
most analysts have serious doubts about the efficiency of earlier
retirements and work-sharing, especially in the short term. It has
been stated above that work-sharing and short time work have been
used in Japan to protect the life time employment system; it has
certainly had favourable effects on the recruitment of new entrants.
A similar proposal was presented for discussion in the EEC paper
"Measures to reduce youth unemployment". However, many argue that
such a proposal presupposes a high degree of substitution and mobility in both external and internal labour markets. If these do not
exist, the proposed measures would be of no significant help in the
context of a cyclical policy. It also presupposes that adult workers
are ready to forgo or share their work for the benefit of the younger
generations, including teenagers. This cannot be official policy and
indeed may well not be accepted by the trade unions.

Measures to maintain employment or to counter unemployment have
no clear-cut effect on young people. On the one hand, measures that
make it difficult for employers to lay off workers may decrease the
instability of young workers and therefore their risks of remaining
unemployed. On the other hand, employers may become more reluctant
to recruit young people if they know that they commit themselves for
the future. On the whole, it would seem that maintaining employment

---

* Cf. "Recommendation of the Council of the OECD on a general employment and manpower policy", Meeting of the OECD Manpower and Social
  Affairs Committee at ministerial level, 4th and 5th March, 1976.

during recessions essentially aims at protecting adult workers at the expense of the younger generations.

General measures to stimulate the whole economy or specific regions or industries have a potentially more important effect on young people. To the extent that these measures succeed in achieving fuller employment, jobs will be made available to all categories of workers, including young people. It can be argued, however, that young workers will be the last category to benefit from a recovery. Nevertheless, when such measures are focussed on specific regions or industries, they are applied regardless of the categories of workers involved and their effects on youth employment can be more promising in the short term. An interesting feature, especially when specific industries are concerned, is that they can be selective in terms of the qualifications required. Some of these measures, for example those favouring research or technologically advanced industries, can provide jobs which correspond to the qualifications of specific categories of young people, for instance graduates in science and technology or trained technicians.

It is not the purpose of this paper to discuss the effects of general measures against unemployment. However, it should be borne in mind that in some cases they may be more effective for certain categories of young people, particularly those who possess saleable skills, than the more specific measures devised essentially for them, which are examined below.

C. SPECIAL MEASURES AGAINST YOUTH UNEMPLOYMENT

OECD countries have considered and implemented a number of measures intended to benefit young people exclusively. Rather than list each country's programmes in detail, the following typology is proposed, presenting measures according to the accessibility they provide to actual employment. Some of these distinguish between new entrants who have not worked before and those who have some work experience.

   a) subsidies, tax credits, or tax exemptions to employers who retain or hire young workers.
   b) the institution of a quota system requiring that a fixed proportion of employees in stipulated enterprises should be below a given age.
   c) changing the redundancy or dismissal payments system to make it more favourable to the retention of young workers.
   d) special efforts to fill existing youth vacancies through information, guidance, placement activities or the payment of mobility allowances.

e) subsidies, tax credits or tax exemptions to employers who agree to train young people.
f) improved subsidised work-study arrangements for those still in educational institutions.
g) occupational training in public training centres, schools, etc.
h) basic education to qualify youth for occupational training.
i) extension of compulsory education.
j) encouragement of young people to extend education voluntarily.
k) job creation for youth by the public authorities in activities that could lead to regular employment.
l) humanitarian, leisure, recreational or diversionary activities at home or abroad, unpaid or low-paid.
m) remedial education in basic cognitive skills.
n) remedial programmes to improve attitudes, behaviour and performance when employment or training are sought or obtained.
o) financial support to unemployed youth, including those who have never worked.

Categories (a)-(d) involve paid activity at a regular work place; categories (e)-(g) are focussed on occupational training, whether in industry, in training centres or through the development of work-study combinations; categories (h)-(j) are methods of temporarily reducing the youth labour supply which may or may not improve ultimate employability; categories (k)-(l) are ways of providing an occupation for unemployed youth, which may or may not lead to regular employment; categories (m)-(n) are specialised services to disadvantaged youth; and category (o) is unemployment pay, a residual measure, an acknowledgement of society's failure to provide either employment or a substitute activity with the potential of leading to employment, although unemployment benefits can enable considered and unhurried search for appropriate re-employment. It should also be noted that unemployment and job changing, particularly voluntary job changing, very often results in improvement in job status.

In practice, the programmes themselves are not always so clearly defined as this list might imply. Combinations of purposes are quite common and a single programme may incorporate elements of remedial education, social services, occupational training and work experience. For purposes of analysis, however, the six major divisions adopted above facilitate consideration of the advantages and disadvantages and the contributions and costs of each major approach toward reducing cyclical youth unemployment.

1. Providing Employment at a regular workplace

The first group of methods (a)-(d), which includes subsidies of various kinds, intensified placement efforts, mobility allowances, and quota systems, is intended to encourage the employment in an actual workplace of young people who otherwise might be unemployed. The following examples are drawn from the range of such measures. In the United Kingdom, the Recruitment Subsidy Scheme was designed to encourage employers to provide more employment opportunities for young people who had recently left school or college by paying them £5 per week for 26 weeks for each recruit. France also has initiated subsidies to employers for the hiring of young people, particularly new entrants: 500 francs per month for 6 months are paid to employers providing at least one year's employment.* In Italy, it is proposed to create 50,000 jobs, in which young people could acquire training and work experience during a one-year period; a monthly salary of 100,000 Italian lire would be paid to the trainees from public funds, so that they would incur no direct cost to the employer. It is envisaged that these trainees have priority for recruitment at the end of this period. Sweden allocated 5 crowns per hour worked to employers recruiting young people**, while a system of incentives for the placement of 16-year olds is being introduced in the Netherlands. The New Zealand Government has introduced a Private Sector Subsidy Scheme; a subsidy of one-third of the direct wage costs with a minimum of $25 per week is payable to employers; this scheme is particularly attractive to employers who engage young workers.

Financial inducements to employers to engage young people may be less costly per employee than public job creation, provided that the subsidy to employers only relates to the additional employees, over and above the previous or normal staff. Thus, the French scheme only applies when additional jobs are created or retiring workers are replaced. In recessions, employers may be tempted to dismiss existing employees and replace them at a lower cost with young people who have been trained in a public centre.

It has been suggested that employers should be subsidised for all young people on their payroll as a means of preventing the dismissal of those who are not subsidised in order to replace them with those who are. Thus, Eisner's proposal that the American government should exempt employers and all employees aged 16-22 from their contribution to the old age pension fund (up to a certain level of earnings)***was estimated to cost about $3 billions a year.[20] It

---

* This scheme also applies to other categories of workers who have been unemployed for more than 6 months.
** And women. The subsidy was 5 SKr up to 1974, and is now 10 Skr/hour.
*** A similar proposal was made in the OECD report Education and working life in modern society.

meant that employers would be subsidised for 85 per cent of the
16-22 year olds whom they were already employing as an inducement to
hire a small additional number of young people who very likely would
constitute less than 10 per cent of the labour force in that age
group. It is doubtful, however, if the amount of the subsidy resulting from tax exemption (11.7 per cent of wages) would be adequate
to attract many employers to the scheme. The Swedish subsidy programme which offered about 35 per cent (but not more than 10 Skr/hour)
of wage costs for additional youth employees was reasonably successful. Since it is difficult to establish in advance the proper level
and form of subsidy needed to attract the desired number of employers,
it is best if the provisions can be altered without elaborate execu-
tive or legislative action.

Although a quota system is often discussed, the only known case
of such provision for youth occurred in Austria in the 1950's when
the demographic factor together with the post-war economic disloca-
tion indicated that a high level of youth unemployment would per-
sist.[21] Quota systems by age group are not popular because they
give the chosen group the impression that they are not normally employable and because a quota favours one group at the expense of
another, possibly as much in need of jobs. One exception is the way
the youth quota was used in Austria to establish additional training
positions within firms.A comparable measure was taken in Yugoslavia in
1968. There, the Industrial Training Period Scheme required employers
to take on young people with a secondary or higher education as trainees. A similar measure has recently been taken in Belgium: young people
must represent at least 1 per cent of the staff in selected firms.
These schemes are generally recognised as useful and effective,
but are designed more to cope with the structural mismatch
between the demand and supply of skills, than with a cyclical situation. However, in all cases the measures take the form of training
schemes. It seems unlikely, however, that they would be acceptable
to either employers or young people if they were to provide regular
employment at a time when most firms are working in conditions of reduced activity and even partial unemployment.

The subsidies or tax exemptions to employers who retain or hire
young workers seem therefore preferable. Some employers may be interested in recruiting additional employees at a lower cost or may
feel encouraged to bring forward recruitments which would otherwise
have been delayed. There is little evidence as to which categories
of young people are affected by such schemes, but it is likely to be
those whose earnings would be on the low side. The target groups
for such measures are, therefore, those who have just finished compulsory education or those with low level skills. Employers generally, however, do not seem to be very enthusiastic about such schemes,

76

although the British one seems to have been reasonably successful. This lack of enthusiasm can be explained by the level of partial unemployment during recessions, which provides a large reserve of underutilised manpower. Employers seem to be much more interested in training support schemes.

Measures such as those taken in France which make it more difficult for employers to lay off workers, or incentives to employers who agree to defer impending redundancies, such as the Temporary Employment Subsidy in the United Kingdom, are not specifically designed to protect youth unemployment. As emphasized above, on the whole they protect adults rather than young workers since they can make the employer more careful when choosing new employees. If specific measures were to be envisaged in favour of young people, they would have a beneficial effect on their stability but would be more likely to redistribute employment than increase it. Another point to be made is that, if these measures do play a social role inasmuch as they protect those adult workers who would otherwise have been dismissed, they may well be socially negative where the young are concerned and they may be criticized as inflationary. They certainly encourage employers to be more wary in their recruitment, at the expense of the less educated, less skilled or socially underprivileged.

Several countries have intensified the information, guidance and placement activities of their employment services and have adopted or improved mobility allowances under the pressure of recession. Although the majority of these measures are not specifically devised for youth, young people nevertheless receive special attention. In fact, in the United States, approximately 40 per cent of the placements made by the United States Employment Services are young people under 22 years of age, although surveys indicate that only 15 per cent of young people find their jobs through the public or private employment agencies. In 1975, Canada instituted mobility allowances for students taking up summer jobs in another area. Italy is preparing measures to provide career advice and placement for new entrants. France has allocated special resources to help young people who have to leave home to find employment and opportunities for training. The United Kingdom has allocated additional funds to its mobility scheme - the Employment Transfer Scheme - and has extended some provisions to young people which were not formerly available to them. The United Kingdom, New Zealand and Sweden have special vocational guidance and placement services to help unemployed youth.

While the filling of vacancies or awarding of mobility allowances is a net contribution, it is likely to be small. In Canada, only about 1 per cent of the workers who move to another area to look for or take a job receive an allowance through the Canada

77

Manpower Mobility Programme (CMMP). Vacancies almost surely will continue to exist along with youth unemployment. The jobs that go begging are, in most cases, those that are unattractive to young people because of the level of pay, nature of the work, or working environment. When the jobs are filled, they are soon vacated, either by leaving or dismissal. In addition, some unfilled jobs are beyond the qualifications of the available unemployed young people or are located in places to which they will not move, even with mobility allowances. In France, it has been noted that young people in Brittany do not make full use of the facilities which they are offered to move to other regions, but that many emigrate to Germany without any governmental help. In view of the successful adjustment of large numbers of unsubsidised migrants, both internally and externally, nations may wish to review the question of which age groups and types of individual should receive mobility allowances.

Measures that aim to provide employment at a regular work place certainly respond to the aspirations of many young people, who do not wish to go back to school or to undertake training. To them a job represents an income, access to individual autonomy and the feeling of being settled in times of high instability. Among young people, other measures (provision of training, temporary occupation, etc.) are considered as valid only when they lead to employment at a regular work place. It seems therefore that such measures are an essential part of an anti-cyclical policy, although they may be less efficient than might be expected.

Quota systems have seldom been adopted during the current recession.Mobility and placement measures,although useful and necessary,have a limited impact on young people when there are not many jobs available that they would accept or for which they are qualified. Mobility allowances may be as much a social measure as an economic instrument. Measures which make dismissals more difficult may be helpful to employed young people who have a saleable skill, since they provide stable employment perspectives and therefore opportunities to grow up in a job. It would seem that such measures would serve the same segments of the youth work force as the subsidies to individual industries considered above. However, they are socially selective and could therefore be harmful to other categories of workers.

Subsidies to employers who recruit young people are much more flexible as a measure. They are used by those who do not have partial unemployment, they increase total employment rather than redistribute it and seem economically viable. Nevertheless, they require careful monitoring to ensure that employers do not dismiss workers when the subsidy ends. It might be unwise to combine these measures systematically with any of those already discussed above. Another difficulty is that the subsidy generally covers a rather short period, whereas the effects of recession on youth will last much longer than the recession itself: although the segmentation of the labour markets may have some impact, the first implication of economic recovery will be the suppression of partial and full-time adult unemployment. It may be asked therefore whether a six months subsidy is sufficient to encourage employers to recruit young workers when in fact they would not reasonably be envisaging recruiting new entrants until some time after the end of recession. A final point is that such programmes or incentives could be used in recessions to integrate into the permanent staff those who were previously working as auxiliary staff, as is currently the practice in many administrations. There would then be no net increase in total employment.

2. Training for Employment

At the present time, there may be a tendency to regard training as something to keep in reserve for young people who might not otherwise be productively employed. At the same time, however, manpower training is rarely intended to be exclusively for youth. In the case of Sweden, the system of labour market training was introduced to satisfy the need for rapid action to counter imbalances in the labour market both by helping under- and unemployed workers to improve their employability in occupations with better opportunities and by increasing the supply of skills in industries where a shortage of suitably trained personnel tends to exacerbate inflationary pressures; furthermore the scheme was designed to contribute towards a greater degree of equality between various groups by supporting those in the weakest position on the labour market. Many such policies are specifically designed for adults, but youth may come to the fore in national programmes, as in France and the United States. In a situation of high unemployment rates for young people, specific programmes may be devised for them.

Measures to maintain the level of training are essentially directed towards on-the-job training - (e) in the list of measures - and the various work-study combinations (f). They are of particular importance in those countries where employers already have considerable responsibility for the training of young people.

In some of these countries, apprenticeship is an essential aspect of industrial training; during recessions, employers tend to reduce their intake of young apprentices, as has been noted in Australia, the United Kingdom and Germany, for example. In the United Kingdom, the number of grants payable for first-year and second-year on-the-job training to employers who offer additional places for apprentices is being increased, and so is the number of grants to selected firms undertaking to train additional apprentices for the full period of four years. There are also provisions for

79

apprentices threatened by redundancy. In Australia, the National
Apprenticeship Assistance Scheme (NAAS) offers subsidies to employers
to meet training costs for apprentices until they are fully productive, providing there are no fewer apprentices than in the preceding
year or they exceed 25 per cent of all the tradesmen on the payroll;
these subsidies were increased in January 1975 as a means of maintaining intakes. The Special Assistance Programme prevents suspen-
sion or cancellation of apprenticeship indentures; it offers special
subsidies for employers providing full-time off-the-job assistance
under the National Employment and Training Scheme (NEAT); and pre-
apprenticeship training via special assistance to trainees under the
NEAT Scheme. On the whole, the tendency is for countries to raise
the budgets or subsidies for apprenticeship programmes as, for
example, in Switzerland or in the special programme in Northern
Ireland.

Such measures may not, however, be sufficient to raise the
number of on-the-job apprenticeships to the desired level, and in
such cases off-the-job training has to be promoted or developed. An
example of this is the Training Awards given to first-year aspiring
apprentices in the United Kingdom to assist them until such time as
they are recruited to an apprenticeship. But on-the-job training
or the various work-study combinations subsidised through such programmes cannot provide training opportunities to all young people
who need them, so training for employment has also to be organised
in public training centres (g), outside the actual labour market.[22]
In Germany, for example, 10,000 additional places will be offered by
the central training shops in 1976.

Policies that aim to promote or develop training opportunities
in public training centres are of particular importance in countries
where preparation for employment takes place principally in formal
classroom situations that are the responsibility of Education and/or
Manpower authorities, or in private institutions of a similar nature.
This is the case in France and in Italy. In countries such as these,
on-the-job training may be considered as somewhat restrictive so far
as individual development is concerned and attempts are being made
to achieve objectives other than those of simple occupational training.

During periods of recession policies tend towards the expansion
of existing programmes. In many cases it may also be necessary to
develop new programmes for young people or to find ways in which
young people can take advantage of the programmes intended for the
adult population.

An example of such new development is the French programme which,
with the co-operation of employers, provides vocational training for
new entrants to the labour market in the form of courses in educational institutions; in 1975 it aimed to provide 50,000 training

places. In Belgium a similar programme has been launched; but this
has involved the creation of a number of special training centres.
In Denmark, a special working party has recommended an increase in
short training courses as a first priority for dealing with massive
youth unemployment: this training is provided in a number of training centres as well as in technical and commercial schools.

In some countries, where employers are held responsible for
training young people, manpower training programmes may in fact ex-
clude teenagers from public training courses. In such countries
the extension of training provisions specifically for young people,
or at least certain categories of them, is to be expected. In the
United Kingdom the Training Opportunities Scheme is open to those
aged 19 or over who have been out of full-time education for at
least three years. The Training Services Agency which runs TOPS
has already provided some courses for young people outside the TOPS
scheme. In the present economic situation the provision of these
training courses for young people under 19 is being expanded. It
has also been agreed that courses will be made available to young
people aged between 19 and 25 who have failed to complete courses
of higher and further education. Only a comparatively small number
of young people leaving the education system (particularly in the
14-19 year age bracket) were considered eligible for all the benefits under the Canadian Manpower Training Programme. These are intended primarily for people who have been in the labour force for at
least one year since leaving school. The programme has now been
supplemented by the "Canada Manpower Industrial Training Programme"
from which many young people without experience will be able to
benefit.

In the United States, the 1974 Comprehensive Employment and
Training Act provides job training and employment opportunities to
the whole work force: however about 60 per cent of the Act's clients
are unemployed young people.

In addition to the development of training opportunities of a
traditional nature, whether on-the-job (e.g. apprenticeships) or in
training centres, some countries have launched innovative schemes
providing a transition between actual schooling and productive employment to facilitate entry into the world of work. In France, the
employment training contract guarantees the young applicant a job
for two years and a vocational training of adaptation to the job
lasting 120 to 500 hours; the courses are given in firms or in training institutions. A subsidy representing 100 per cent of the minimum
industrial wage is granted to employers during the course itself and
30 per cent of this wage for the period not spent on the course.
In Belgium the State grants financial assistance to employers who
offer a training period to young school and university graduates on

their first employment; this period allows them to adapt themselves
in the firm to tasks related to their previous studies. The first
six months are devoted solely to training, during which period the
State pays a part of the trainee's wages (equivalent to unemployment
benefits). These measures, which are designed for young people between 16 and 25 in France, and 15 and 25 in Belgium, appear to be
much more flexible than company training or apprenticeship schemes
because they cover a much broader range of skills and levels. The
United Kingdom intends to introduce an experimental programme, beginning in September 1976 and lasting for at least two or three
years, under which a variety of pilot schemes of unified further education and training, termed 'vocational preparation', will be tested
and evaluated. This programme is aimed at improving current provision for the 16-19 age-group, particularly those entering employment other than at craft level. It is intended that at least 20
schemes will be set up. The duration of courses within the schemes
may vary but an average of 12 weeks full-time or part-time equivalent
is envisaged. It is expected that the number of young people for
whom provision will be made will rise to about 6,000 per annum. Decisions on the nature and location of schemes will take account of
the levels of youth unemployment, current rates of participation in
post-school education, the need to ensure a geographical spread and
to cover a range of industries and occupations, and local interest,
facilities and other circumstances. In addition to the education
and training authorities, other interested bodies such as employers'
organisations, trade unions and youth organisations will be invited
to participate in the planning and development of pilot schemes.
The main aims of these courses of vocational preparation will be to
assist young people:

    i) to assess their potential and think realistically about jobs
       and careers;
   ii) to develop the basic skills which will be needed in adult
       life, generally;
  iii) to understand their society and how it works;
   iv) to strengthen the foundation of skill and knowledge on which
       further training and education can be built.

    The current costs of the pilot schemes will be met from central
government funds. Young participants not in employment will be
eligible for training allowances at the rates currently applicable
to courses run by the training agency of the Manpower Services
Commission. Those in employment should suffer no loss of wages.

    It may well be felt that training measures, in particular those
that relate to the development of public training courses, cannot be
expanded rapidly. On the other hand, it is much easier to find

teachers in times of recession. However, the Swedish experience in setting up temporary training centres during high unemployment, and the French experience in using the support of existing vocational and technical education facilities, show that opportunities can be exploited to the desired level with considerably less difficulty than some have expected.

In the case of training schemes that require the co-operation of industry, it is obviously easier for governments to deal with employers in countries where they are co-operative, as in Scandanavia and the United Kingdom, or where a strong tradition of employer responsibility for training young workers exists, as in Germany. But in all countries it is important to select the employers for these programmes carefully, since those who volunteer most quickly to receive subsidies have often proved the least satisfactory with respect to the quality and type of training and the employment they provide. The size of the firm, as well as its field of commercial or industrial concern, should be taken into account before subsidies are awarded; it may indeed be better to reject some than to place young people in situations where the training is poor, or skills that are not in short supply are provided or the work required is menial and leads nowhere. Supervision of employers' performance is required even after they have been carefully selected. As with employment subsidy schemes, particular attention must be given to inducing net additions to the payroll and to maintaining employment after the subsidy ends. The timing of programmes involving employers is also important; if a programme is launched at a moment when employers are pessimistic about future prospects, the response may be so poor that the programme lapses to a state from which it cannot be revived when prospects begin to improve.

A major policy issue is the types and levels of training on which the main emphasis should be placed. Broadly speaking, there is always a risk that policies aimed at developing existing facilities, programmes or institutions will not respond to the major maladjustments between the characteristics of the youth work force and the likely requirements of the labour market when the recession ends. There must be real skill shortages in the economy if manpower training is to have a counter-cyclical function. A first problem is therefore to identify such shortages or the current weaknesses of the whole training system. The UK Government and the Manpower Services Commission published a consultative document in July 1976 which proposes a means of ensuring that there are enough skilled workers to meet industry's vital needs. The document suggests that a system of collective funding should be set up, whereby some of the costs of initial training should be met by industry and government, rather than by individual employers. The resulting increase in the level of training will mean more young people will have an opportunity to obtain skilled employment.

The next question to be considered is whether policies should concentrate on those unemployed young people who are the most likely to benefit from their training and obtain satisfactory employment; or should they serve the less able and the less qualified, at the risk of being less efficient? On this point, those in charge of training policies may have different views from those in charge of the whole cyclical policy, who launch a comprehensive set of measures, some of them being more expressly directed at the less advantaged. In many countries, there are specific programmes for the less privileged which supplement the actual training programmes, as will be seen presently.

In cases where emphasis has been placed on courses of a short duration, it is likely that trainees will return to the labour market before the recession ends, and may well become unemployed again. It is important therefore that wherever possible such short courses be either related to identified skill shortages on the local labour market; or linked with a longish-term employment contract. In cases where emphasis is placed on longer-term courses, the danger, as has already been pointed out, is that the training will be stopped when the subsidy ends; in cases where employers enter into a contract to provide a full apprenticeship training, they may still be reluctant to recruit young trainees.

It appears that, when mismatches have been identified between the needs of the labour market and the occupational preparation of the young generation, policies may well focus on specific types and levels of training, through institutional development and budget allocation. Another policy is to set up flexible schemes, that may be used and adapted to individual needs (e.g. the French training-employment contract), or to local and regional situations (e.g. the various programmes under the Comprehensive Employment and Training Act in the United States).

Recent experience shows that a major obstacle to the efficient implementation of training programmes lies in the attitudes and aspirations of the young people concerned. Many of the unemployed are reluctant to enter training courses, especially in public centres, because they are uneasy about the possibility of missing an opportunity for re-employment and doubtful about their chances in a new field. With new entrants, additional difficulties have to be faced. Many young people, particularly those who are prone to unemployment, have developed rejection attitudes towards education and are not willing to undertake further training, particularly in off-the-job training centres. They just do not believe that such further training will improve their chances of finding a job. Many young people, too, refuse to undertake a training in which they have no interest and which might lead to jobs they would not accept. Such people may prefer to remain unemployed, particularly in those countries where they are entitled to unemployment benefits, and find themselves in an increasingly marginal situation. Such attitudes often explain the frequent lack of success of training programmes and the low utilisation of the budgets allocated to them.

An important issue here is the proper level of incentives that should be offered, directly or indirectly, to young people during their period of training. In most countries, allowances are linked to training programmes. They have to be high enough to actually attract young people; but they cannot be reasonably decided without regard to other established benefits, such as the unemployment allowance, the wages paid to apprentices, the indemnities which sometimes may or may not be paid to vocational-technical trainees.

It seems generally to be the case that on-the-job training programmes are more successful in attracting young people than courses in public centres. As already pointed out, young people who are willing to undertake training are primarily interested in a job, and many have doubts about employment prospects at the conclusion. However they are clearly more confident in their chances when they are trained at an actual place of work.

3. Temporary Reductions in the Youth Labour Force

Another method of coping with recession unemployment among young people involves their temporary removal from the labour force by attracting them to some kind of further education. This might take the form of: extension of compulsory education (i); basic education to qualify youth for occupational training (h); encouragement for them to stay on longer, and voluntarily, at school (j).

If, irrespective of youth unemployment conditions, a prior public decision has been made to extend compulsory education, it is clearly advantageous to introduce it during a recession so that the initial withdrawal of a number of young people from the labour market will reduce the unemployment rate. In the Netherlands, the implementation of compulsory schooling for 15-year olds has been accelerated for both educational and manpower reasons and it became effective in August 1975. The introduction of the second day of full-time compulsory education for 16-year olds will be accompanied by a temporary financial incentive scheme to employers who must release the young people from work.

In Germany there are preparatory courses preceding vocational training as well as courses for improving the placing and resettling prospects of juveniles who still lack the maturity to enter a recognised occupation. There are, too, basic training courses for unemployed young people. Another example is to be found in New Zealand where courses are provided in areas where employment is scarce. Both schemes aim at preventing potential unemployment and at providing pre-vocational training leading to proper vocational training.

Another recession move is to encourage potentially unemployed young people to continue education voluntarily through financial subsidies from the government, which may find the cost of this less than the unemployment insurance that otherwise would have to be paid. This approach has been used in Canada, although it may not have been an explicit policy; it is questioned currently, and additional education is no longer considered as an automatic passport to better jobs. In Australia, young people return to school or a higher level of studies because of difficulty in obtaining employment. No official programme has encouraged young people to prolong their education as an alternative to unemployment; nevertheless, a higher proportion of students than usual has recently returned to full-time studies. In 1975, re-enrolments at secondary level have been up to an estimated 10 per cent higher than was expected on the basis of past trends. In the United Kingdom those about to leave school are being encouraged to stay on at school or to enter further education, if the alternative is a period of unemployment. It may also be that the pressure to extend the duration of studies in selected vocational schools in Italy (although motivated by the upgrading of the training given in order to provide access to universities) can be interpreted in the same way - the schools acting as a parking place for young people who otherwise would be unemployed. In Ireland no inducements are being offered to encourage young people to stay on at school, but a scheme is to be introduced whereby people under 25 who are unemployed can take a training course of 9 or 15 months' duration in one of the Regional Technical Colleges and be paid an allowance of £9 per week.

While additional education in recession periods temporarily removes job seekers from the labour market, it can result in greater difficulty later on, especially if it creates expectations that the labour market cannot fulfil. Extension of compulsory education during a recession has a short but massive effect on reducing youth unemployment. Basic education, which qualifies for occupational training, can help less-privileged young people compensate for their disadvantages and it can improve their working life. Prolongation of voluntary education may do more harm than good if it is not relevant to labour market needs; recent experience, particularly in the United States, shows that students, who in the past tended to accumulate degrees and diplomas until they were judged over-qualified for the job available, today tend to select courses more relevant to the world of work.

4. Job Creation

Another traditional instrument of anti-cyclical policy in times of recession is to launch employment development schemes, labour intensive projects, such as public works. In addition to such general measures, specific job-creation programmes may be designed or developed. However, job creation explicitly for youth is less common than job-creation programmes that have a youth section or large scale participation by young people. Among these programmes, a distinction may be made between job creation that could lead to regular employment (k) and humanitarian, recreational or social service activities (1).

In times of recession, a number of countries lift the ceiling on full-time staff employment in the public services; in Australia, for example, provisions have been made specifically for an additional intake of young recruits and trainees.* As already noted, the problem with such measures is that they may be used for the integration of auxiliary staff already working in the public service and hence make no real addition to total employment.

Within the public relief programme in Denmark the Government appropriated a specific budget for youth while the Local Employment Assistance in Canada only has 12 per cent of persons under 20 among its clients. Although these programmes cover a variety of activities, most of them offer occupational jobs that come close to those in regular employment.

The Canadian Opportunities for Youth Programme provided summer jobs for young people: in 1974, half of the funded projects had a recreational or social service character, the rest were cultural, educational or environmental. More recently a job-creation programme has been developed in the United Kingdom and covers work projects of social value, while the Netherlands Government is subsidising new projects in health care work and socio-cultural activities for the benefit of unemployed people in the 15-22 age group. The Italian Government proposes to undertake specific projects of social interest: inventory of artistic treasures, revision of the land registry, forestry work, etc., to provide occupations for unemployed youngsters. In Canada, the Local Initiative Programme, which was not exclusively designed for young people, the proportion participating was high in comparison to their labour force shares.

Such programmes, as well as the various American programmes (from the Civilian Conservation Corps in the '30s to more recent programmes for out of school and in school) exemplify job-creation

---

* However in this context it is necessary to keep in mind the ceilings that have been subsequently imposed on federal public service employment, the most recent of which require a reduction in some government departments, despite the current recession.

measures; but social objectives beyond furnishing useful employment may also be present. Many are directed to less advantaged young people who, even in times of high employment, might have difficulty in finding jobs.

The difference between programmes such as the Peace Corps and job creation focussed on the regular employment market is one of degree, but the skills acquired in the humanitarian type of programmes are the more difficult to convert into paid jobs or careers. For some unemployed young people, such programmes are the most valuable use of idle time that could be devised, but for the most part they seem to interest those who, having other options, use the experience to bridge educational courses, to "find themselves" or, in the case of adults, to make a change of career or occupy retirement time. In general, programmes organised for job creation are more effective for the young unemployed than the humanitarian ones.

In Part I, some of the difficulties posed by job-creation programmes have been outlined. The Canadian Authorities emphasized that about half of the projects under their LIP programme provided products or services for which no alternatives existed in the communities involved. In cases where it provided a supplementary (a potentially competing) product or service for which alternatives did exist, there were strong indications that the communities' needs were often not altogether met by the existing network of services.[23]

Another issue is the nature of the jobs offered by such programmes. Many job-creation programmes are labour intensive, and may therefore provide employment opportunities that many young people may not wish to accept. It was noted in Denmark, for example, that young people engaged in the public relief programme considered their tasks could have been more efficiently performed by heavy equipment or machinery. Many such programmes are in fact directed towards the less privileged, less qualified youth; however, these young people are already more educated and better informed than the average members of the work force. They have to be motivated by the cultural or social purpose of the programmes.

Public job creation on a large scale gives rise to a number of other issues. In the case of young people, there is disagreement as to whether job creation or training is the more useful.[24] Over the whole field one can observe conflicts between providing the largest possible number of created jobs and offering fewer well-paid jobs, and between serving the most employable individuals (who will move more easily from created jobs to regular employment) and aiding those who have chronic difficulty in competing for jobs. Thus, counter-cyclical and human resource development goals may not coincide. The type of jobs to be created, the degree of training incorporated in the job and the duration of the jobs are other aspects requiring decisions.[25] Despite their intentions, job-creation programmes have a poor record on transfers to regular jobs. As against training, created jobs generally are more expensive, promise little current or future contribution to market output, are more difficult to organise effectively, and are hard to terminate before regular employment is obtained.

In addition, most anti-cyclical measures and job-creation programmes are designed on the assumption of a return to full employment. Recent discussions* show that in most countries it will be extremely difficult to come back to a full employment situation in the near future; as far as young people are concerned, it has already been noted in this paper that employment prospects may not be as favourable as they have been in the past. It may therefore be that job-creation programmes will have to be continued in some way on a permanent basis. This has many implications in terms of choice of activities, duration of individual indentures and the mix of social categories among the youth population.

5. Programmes for Disadvantaged Youth

The remedial programmes for the disadvantaged, (m) and (n) in the list of measures, are not essentially counter-cyclical, although they may be expanded in recession periods because more of their potential clients are visibly unemployed. Most remedial programmes are not designed exclusively for young people, although there are cases of specific schemes for young people, such as the Community Industry Scheme in the United Kingdom.

In times of recession, rehabilitation programmes for the handicapped may be extended. However, from a review of the measures taken in the countries, it would seem that policy emphasis is on the protection or the employment of those who are more socially disadvantaged than the physically handicapped. More relevant to this discussion are the programmes designed for those who have cultural, social or other disadvantages, for example schemes for improving the linguistic performance of migrant workers.

As far as young people are concerned, it may be easier to recognise potential clients for courses in periods of recession; but they will certainly be more sceptical about what they can gain from them than they would be at times when jobs, however poor, are available. The objective should be to help the less able to compensate for their disadvantages in periods during which they are likely to be unemployed, to provide allowances during the scheme, and to improve their position on the labour market when the economy recovers.

_____
* Meeting of Ministers of Labour held in OECD, 4th and 5th March, 1976.

Programmes for the disadvantaged cover a variety of schemes: experience of work with one or several employers, job creation*, basic education and training. In many cases emphasis is placed on education and training. However, in most countries, programmes are not explicitly directed towards disadvantaged young people as such; the set of measures adopted attempts, rather, to deal with the specific problems of the various categories of young people on the basis of a technical analysis of individual situations, and avoids singling out so-called disadvantaged people, who might otherwise be made to feel increasingly marginal.

6. Unemployment Payments

Financial support for young people who have lost their jobs is usually part of the general system for coping with unemployment. Young people, eligible for unemployment insurance or unemployment allowances on the same terms as adults, may, however, be at a disadvantage if they have not accumulated sufficient weeks of work to qualify for such insurance benefit. Belgium, Switzerland and France are unusual in granting unemployment benefits in their own right to eligible young people who have never worked. For the new entrant in other countries, financial support during unemployment is either non-existent or is provided as an outcome of the family support system. Family allowances and dependents' allowances under unemployment insurance and unemployment allowances usually disqualify young people as dependents when they leave school because it is assumed that those living at home will get jobs and will contribute all or part of their earnings to the family. When such young people do not find work after leaving school, there is a family income problem, especially if the chief breadwinner is also unemployed. To deal with this problem, unemployed school leavers are permitted to draw welfare, unemployment assistance or (in the United Kingdom) supplementary benefits in their own right.

Financial support is a residual measure which it is better to replace by other methods. Belgium has proposed that a certain number of the young recipients of its unemployment benefits should receive six months of training from employers. The young people would continue to receive their unemployment benefits and the employer would pay to the government all the social security contributions and taxes related to the employment. Other countries also have tried to make more productive use of the time of young people who receive financial support during unemployment.

---

* In New Zealand work is provided to young persons who have poor employment records in the Work Adjustment Centres operated by the Rehabilitation League; during their period of attachment, efforts are made to find permanent employment for the participants.

D. PROBLEMS RAISED BY COUNTER-CYCLICAL YOUTH POLICY

To face the current recession and sometimes the additional difficulties created by population changes, most OECD countries have
launched a set of specific measures against youth unemployment. Temporary measures had already been taken by Sweden in the period
1972-1974. Some countries, such as Norway, have suffered less from
the recession; others, such as Japan, with a different employment
system, have placed more emphasis on safeguarding the employment of
older workers. National policies provide various combinations of
the measures that have been listed and discussed above; emphasis
varies from country to country. In the United Kingdom, for instance,
more importance is attached to training; in Denmark to public relief
works and job creation.

These policies raise a number of problems. Their success de-
pends on the mix of the programme, the efficiency of their administration and the actual motivation of participants. There seems to
be no reason to believe that young people gain less from such measures than other age groups. However, in some European countries,
the recession brought to light a youth problem for which the existing
institutions were not prepared and new mechanisms, new approaches
and a new co-ordination between education and manpower authorities
are required, while in other countries, such as Sweden, it may be
enough for existing programmes to be adapted or reinforced.

As already pointed out, some of the measures under consideration
are potentially harmful to other categories of workers. Not so however in the case of some recent legislation for employment protection,
in countries such as France, Sweden, the United Kingdom, Germany,
where dismissal is being made increasingly difficult for the employer.
This actually favours adult employment, to the extent that the efficiency of the measures taken with regard to youth come into question. Broadly speaking, general measures against unemployment, or
in support of employment protection, lead employers to be more wary
when recruiting young people, thus increasing the disadvantages of
those who are less trained and less skilled.

A more difficult problem is to evaluate the inflationary effect
of different measures. If very stringent anti-inflationary measures
are adopted, many of the specific programmes to reduce unemployment
will be difficult to operate, and in some cases this leaves income
maintenance as a better alternative. However, the inflationary effects of individual measures or programmes are not always clear,
especially over time.

This leads to a difficult political choice. If general measures
to combat unemployment induce employers to be more selective, and
if the set of measures for youth is designed in terms of its effects

91

on inflation or future productivity, it is clear that the programme will favour those young people who are more able, more adaptable and more trainable at the expense of those who are less advantaged. The latter will have to be covered by unemployment allowances, or encouraged to remain in school. At the other extreme, and at the risk of being inefficient, youth policy may concentrate on the less privileged, both at the individual and national level. A compromise could, of course, be made by helping the less-trained to compensate for their disadvantages, while offering increased development opportunities to the more able, but the financial situation may not allow this. National policies differ so far as these choices are concerned, and it may be that the matter has not always receive the fullest consideration, because of political pressures on governments. It is likely however that a review of the spending of youth programme budgets would show that the first of the two strategies is usually the more successful. Nevertheless, some groups may have a very low priority in terms of government programmes.

One difficulty of a counter-cyclical policy, as outlined above, is to cover the whole of the recession period. It has also been pointed out that the economic upturn will first be used to reabsorb the partial and full-time adult unemployment and that employment difficulties for young people will continue for some time longer. A set of measures providing training, employment or diversionary activities for only six months or so would therefore be quite inadequate, although it might help to dampen the effects of the arrival of new candidates for employment at the end of the academic year. In the United Kingdom, subsidies for first-year apprentices are today supplemented by subsidies for the second year. In France, the initial period for the employment training contract has had to be extended. In all cases the time perspective is essential in framing effective policies. Relevant to this discussion are the problems raised by the annual flood of young people, particularly those under 20, into the work force at the end of the school year. During the summer, the teenage labour force generally rises by about 40 per cent in the United States, and unemployment nearly doubles. This seasonal flow brings forth a major policy response in the United States, where about 1 million summer work experience jobs are created for young people. In Canada, special arrangements are made to help absorb the flood of students, mainly through the Opportunities for Youth Programme. In Europe, attention is less focussed on summer employment for students than on the effects of the arrival of young people leaving full time education on the employment situation; these effects are at their peak in September/October, after the holiday period. It is to be feared that one main concern of governments short term policy is to dampen the effects of this seasonal flow and to prevent a sudden rise in youth unemployment. Such a concern may lead them to devise measures and programmes that are too limited in scope and too short in duration to cope with the cyclical dimension of youth unemployment.

As already noted, many young people prefer work to training, especially if training is not on an employer's premises, and this feeling is accentuated when they do not feel particularly confident about the future. However, activities at the work place can only take care of some of the young people unemployed. This raises the question of the comparative levels of incentive: wages to apprentices, training allowances, starting salaries in created jobs and unemployment benefits, when they exist. It also brings up the attitudes and reactions of young people towards the various opportunities being offered, that finally determine the success or failure of youth policies. This however may be primarily a structural question, and this will be examined below.

III. CONONJUNCTURAL MEASURES IN STRUCTURAL PERSPECTIVE

No matter how effective the short-term programmes to reduce youth unemployment may be, they cannot be fully satisfactory for two major reasons. First, the basic assumption of anti-cyclical policy is that the economy can return to full employment and to the structural relationships which prevailed before the recession. It also disregards structural changes in the economy that alter job opportunities and the relative position of various groups in the labour market. The second drawback of short-term policy is that it necessarily concentrates on youth unemployment to the neglect of other issues of a longer-term character affecting the entry and establishment of young people in working life. Short-term policies also tend to make too few differentiations among young people.

In the first part of this report, a number of issues of a structural nature have been identified. Even in more favourable periods, the transition from school to working life seems increasingly difficult for a significant number of young people. It is not easy to evaluate the precise proportion of youth in each country who suffer from the difficulties outlined in Part I, but it may be as high as a third in some countries. This figure was cited a few years ago in the Manpower Report of the President of the United States for young people with no more than an upper secondary education. Analysis shows that the current recession multiplies the effects of existing imbalances and reveals structural shortcomings.

A combination and harmonisation of short-term and longer-term policies in education and employment seems to be called for. This raises the problem of the convergence of the specific measures discussed above and the longer-term policies required by the structural situation.

A. WHAT CYCLICAL MEASURES ARE APPROPRIATE
TO THE STRUCTURAL SITUATION?

Not all the specific measures discussed above are of a conjunctural nature. Special efforts to fill existing vacancies through information, guidance and placement activities, remedial education for the less advantaged, for example, represent an extension of existing services, that are there to deal with problems arising in the structural area. Such measures as the extension of compulsory education, or changes in the dismissal payments system, will be maintained when the recession ends. Also, some programmes such as job creation or public relief work are considered as cyclical, although they may have to be continued after the recession, if, for example, full employment cannot be reached. Below, the emphasis is placed on short-term action.

Recent experience in France shows that enrolments in youth programmes are sometimes far below the expected level. Actual expenditures for some such measures represent only one third of the appropriations. Of course, where subsidised employment or on-the-job training are concerned, this may be explained by the attitudes of employers, who during recessions are reluctant to recruit additional staff or trainees or by poor preparation and administration of hastily adopted laws. However, the lack of success of public relief activities or off-the-job training must be linked with young people's attitudes and lack of participation, as pointed out in a recent Danish report. However, Sweden has no difficulty in recruiting for programmes which are well-conceived.

The analysis in Part I clearly shows that these attitudes are the result of the mismatch between young people's expectations, their occupational preparation, the nature of the jobs being offered and prevailing working conditions. During the current recession, in some countries there are still vacancies at all levels of skills, and employers complain about manpower shortages. While many young people are unwilling to take the existing jobs opportunities, they will clearly not be attracted either by training activities that may lead to these jobs or by created jobs of a comparable nature.

In such circumstances, financial incentives may not be enough to attract young people into employment or training. In the first place, the proportion with such negative attitudes, or with no skill at all, is likely to be much higher among those who are not unemployed. Also, many young people in developed countries are economically able to remain idle. The financial incentives offered are, of course, much below the salary of an established job, and young people may well prefer to await better opportunities. In some countries, e.g. Canada, cultural interests or the will to be socially useful may attract a number of young people into special programmes, but these are of little interest as a preparation for entry later into working life.

A large segment of the youth population, which includes all those with more than compulsory education, is interested in employment at a regular work place, in so-called career jobs, or in a long term training which may lead to challenging jobs. It should be emphasized here that manpower shortages in some countries do not apply only to menial jobs, but also to well-paid, fully respected occupations that require prior qualification. Considering both young people's aspirations and the qualifications needed for a wide range of jobs, there is undoubtedly room for measures that encourage the acquisition of high level skills.

The development of long term training is not always relevant to cyclical policy. However, examples can be cited of incentives to apprenticeship or long term on-the-job training to maintain the system in operation, that have a cyclical character. Creating such training opportunities is expensive, and cutbacks in public expenditure may not allow their extension on a wide scale. In such conditions, encouraging young people to remain at school or university may be useful as a measure to reduce numbers in the work force temporarily, but it may be dangerous in the long run if it increases young people's expectations and is not relevant to employment needs.

Short term training, which has been successfully used by traditional manpower policies, does not seem to be particularly effective with the better educated segment of the work force. However, some specific categories of young people in the work force can benefit from short term action: some can qualify for occupational training, as in Germany; graduates can be helped to adapt to specific functions through a training period in industry, as in Belgium, or through supplementary courses, as proposed in Denmark. Many can acquire basic skills through accelerated training. Job-creation or subsidised work experience can be used to acquire skills and improve work attitudes.

Among the unemployed, many have left the education system with little occupational training and new entrants from compulsory education are at a particular disadvantage in this respect. Not all will be willing or able to participate in short term programmes. Cyclical policy cannot change the main features or cope with the main deficiencies of the education and training system; it has, therefore, clear limitations. It would seem that it is most useful when it concentrates on identified structural imbalances that are amenable to short term action. This may restrict the scope of cyclical measures as such, and they will have to be supplemented by measures that relate more to the structure of employment and education.

B. WHAT STRUCTURAL MEASURES ARE RELEVANT TO THE CYCLICAL SITUATION?

A number of the measures already discussed above are in fact structural in character. An example is the extension of compulsory education, a measure that reduces the number of young people in the

work force. Measures to assist the placement and mobility of young
people, services for the disadvantaged can also be classified as
structural, although they tend to be reinforced during recession
periods.

Among the measures taken or being considered by OECD Member
countries, one proposal seems particularly relevant: the organisation
of innovative transition periods between school and working life.
The difficulties faced by a high proportion of teenagers during
periods of near full employment are increased considerably during recessions. New schemes such as the French employment training contract
may ease the process of transition for these young people by providing a combination of actual work and study relevant to occupational
life over a period covering the whole of the recession. Such schemes
are obviously relevant both to the cyclical and structural situation
and are of particular importance in those countries where on-the-job
training has no broad extension or where apprenticeship is on the
decline.

Another proposal that merits further consideration is job creation. Today many countries consider that it will be difficult to return to a situation of full employment in the near future. Some of
them believe that a new concept of full employment will have to be
developed to meet the demands of those who wish to work. It is clear
in this perspective that job creation may become a major policy instrument, and the issue is of particular interest where young people
are concerned.

So far most job creation or public relief activities have been
considered as temporary, occasional, cyclical measures. Experience
shows that it is difficult to bring such activities to an end.

C. RELATION OF CONJUNCTURAL TO STRUCTURAL MEASURES

Perhaps the onus should not be on cyclical policy to lead the
structural, but the other way around. If in good times a country can
establish a varied and strong set of programmes to cope with its
structural problems, then in times of recession such measures can be
maintained and, where appropriate, expanded. This will leave to the
cyclical programmes the residual task of caring for those who cannot
be accommodated by the structural measures. If such strong measures
do not exist, the cyclical programmes, which in recession admittedly
get support more easily than structural ones, may tend to treat part
of the structural problem as conjunctural, using policies that do not
contribute to structural solutions. Because it is difficult to start
up structural programmes that rely on employers if there is a recession, the initiative for such programmes should preferably be taken
when near full employment prevails.

In order to deal successfully with the actual employment problems, particularly as far as young people are concerned, it seems that the countries, according to their own situation and particularities, should make some realistic choices. Firstly, they should examine what measures could be taken in the current recession period in relation to the structural issues identified, including the changing behaviour, attitudes and motivations of young people. Another problem is to identify the measures which could be implemented rapidly, whatever their nature, cyclical or structural. But the choice of priorities should keep in mind the complementarity of cyclical and structural measures in relation to the needs of the various groups of young people. In this last respect, it seems that, so far, even when they are especially designed for young people, measures are conceived as general and do not apply specifically to precise categories of school leavers or job seekers.

The current situation shows that it is no longer possible to rely entirely upon market mechanisms to ensure the smooth transition of young people from studies to working life. The question which arises is to what extent governments can adopt measures which reflect an acknowledgement of greater public responsibility for the development of all young people beyond the compulsory school-leaving age, at least until the age of legal majority. There are signs that a number of countries are taking initiatives in this direction, in recognition of the fact that the problems facing young people are essentially structural in nature, and therefore call for corresponding policies conceived in structural terms. This could perhaps overcome the problem of what, if any, priority should be accorded to youth unemployment in times of recession.

REFERENCES

1. Commission of the European Communities, "Measures to Reduce Youth Unemployment",SEC (75) 1706, Brussels, May 1975, Annex, p. 1.

2. Monthly Labor Review, July 1975, pp. 78,79; Manpower Report of the President, 1975, Table B-7.

3. Paul O. Flaim, "Discouraged workers and changes in unemployment", Monthly Labor Review, March 1973, pp. 8-16; Sweden, Central Statistical Bureau (SCB), The development of the labor force resources 1965-1972 and 1972-1980, No. 7, 1973, pp. 61,62; U.S. Department of Labor, Bureau of Labor Statistics, Employment and Earnings, quarterly surveys of Discouraged Workers.

4. Joyanna Moy and Constance Sorrentino, "Unemployment in Nine Industrial Nations, 1973-75", Monthly Labor Review, June 1975, pp. 13-14.

5. William G. Bowen and T. Aldrich Finegan, The Economics of Labor Force Participation, Princeton: Princeton University Press, 1969, ch. 13,14. New York Times, September 3, 1975, "About Education", indicates that high unemployment continues to result in higher enrolments in educational institutions than might otherwise occur.

6. T. Vietorisz, R. Mier and J. Giblin, "Subemployment: exclusion and inadequacy indexes", Monthly Labor Review, May 1975, pp. 3-24; Carolyn Shaw Bell, "Should Every Job Support a Family?" Public Interest, Summer 1975, pp. 109-118; Sar A. Levitan and Robert Taggart, "Employment-earnings inadequacy: a measure of welfare", Monthly Labor Review, October 1973, pp. 19-27; Herman P. Miller, "Subemployment in poverty areas of large U.S. cities", Monthly Labor Review, October 1973, pp. 10-18; William Spring, Bennett Harrison and Thomas Vietorisz, "Crisis of the Underemployed", New York Times Magazine, November 5, 1972; Helen Ginsburg, Unemployment, Subemployment, and Public Policy, New York: New York University School of Social Work, 1975, Part Five.

7. Great Britain, Department of Employment, <u>Unqualified, Untrained and Unemployed</u>, London: HMSO, 1974, pp. 10-11; Great Britain, Manpower Services Commission, <u>There's Work to be done</u>, London: HMSO, 1974, pp. 8, 22-23, 30, 38-40, 44-45; Commission of the European Communities, "Measures to Reduce Youth Unemployment", SEC (75) 1706/2, Brussels, May 1975, Graphs 3B, 3C; A. Pulkkinen, "Entry into the labour market of young people who have finished their studies" (Finland), Table 5, in <u>Entry of young people into working life - Technical reports</u> (forthcoming):Sweden, Central Statistical Bureau (SCB), <u>The development of the labor force resources 1965-1972 and 1972-1980</u>, No. 7, 1973, pp. 49-50; Sweden, Ministry of Labor, <u>Youth and Work</u> (II), Ds. A 1974: 7, Stockholm, 1974, pp. 15-18.

8. <u>Manpower Report of the President</u>, 1975, Tables A3 and A15; U.S. Council of Economic Advisers, <u>Economic Report of the President</u>, 1974, Washington: GPO, 1974, p. 60; George M. Perry, "Changing Labor Markets and Inflation", <u>Brookings Papers on Economic Activity</u>, 1970, No. 3, pp. 441-48; Carolyn Shaw Bell, "The Economics of Might Have Been", <u>Monthly Labor Review</u>, November 1974, pp. 40-42; Steven P. Zell, "The Economics that Never Was", <u>Monthly Labor Review</u>, July 1975, pp. 39-40.

9. Joanna Moy and Constance Sorrentino, "Unemployment in Nine Industralized Nations, 1973-75", <u>Monthly Labor Review</u>, June 1975, p. 13; Curtis L. Gilroy, "Supplemental Measures of Labor Force Underutilization", <u>Monthly Labor Review</u>, May 1975, pp. 16-19.

10. <u>New York Times</u>, May 4, 1975, "The Teen-age Worker is Hardest Hit"; <u>Manpower Report of the President</u>, 1975, Table B-7; OECD, Directorate of Social Affairs, Manpower, and Education, G. Martinoli, "Réflexions sur les rapports entre éducation et emploi dans une perspective italienne (SME/ET/75.10).

11. Le Monde, March 18, 21, 1975, "Cinq cent mille jeunes en quête d'emploi", F.R. Germany, Bundesanstalt für Arbeit, <u>Zur Situation der Arbeitslosigkeit der Jugendlichen</u>, ANBA No. 3, 1975, Nürnberg March 1975, Tables 6, 7; <u>Bestandsaufnahme und kritische Analyse sowie Vorschläge für Massnahmen zum Abbau der Arbeitslosigkeit Jugendlicher und zur Verbesserung der Lage auf dem Aushildungsstellenmarkt</u>, Nürnberg, January 1975, IIa3-6170/4421/5300/5530/5580/8000, Tables 6a, b, c; <u>Erklarung der Bundesregierung zur Jugendarbeitslosigkeit und Ausbildungsstellensituation</u>, Bonn, no date, ubersicht 2.

12. Commission of the European Communities, "Measures to Reduce Youth Unemployment", Annex, p. 4; Graphs 2a, b, c.

13. Great Britain, Department of Employment, Employment News, May 1975, p. 1; Le Monde, May 19, 1975, "Le chômage des jeunes, s'il présente des aspects inquiétants ne doit pas non plus être sur-évalué"; Great Britain, Department of Employment, Unqualified, Untrained and Unemployed, Appendix 6; Great Britain, Department of Employment, Final Triennial Report by the National Youth Employment Council, London: HSMO, 1974, p. 24; Beatrice G. Reubens, Bridges to Work: International Comparisons of Transition Services (forthcoming).

14. Great Britain, Department of Employment, Employment Prospects for the Highly Qualified, Manpower Papers No. 8, London: HMSO, 1974.

15. See forthcoming study by Manfred Tessaring and Heinz Werner, F.R. Germany, Bundesanstalt für Arbeit, Institut für Arbeitsmarkt- and Berufsforschung; Wirtschaftswoche, May 9, 1975, pp. 48-54; Heinz Werner, "Beschäftigungsprobleme von Akademikern", Wirtschaftsdienst, No. III, 1975, pp. 146-150.

16. Beatrice G. Reubens, "Vocational Education for All in High School?" in James O'Toole, ed., Work and the Quality of Life, Cambridge: M.I.T. Press, 1974; Beverly Duncan, "Dropouts and the Unemployed", Journal of Policital Economy, 1964, pp. 121-134; Margaret Plunkett, "School and Early Work Experience of Youth", Occupational Outlook Quarterly, No. 1, 1960, pp. 22-27.

17. Great Britain, Unqualified, Untrained and Unemployed, pp. 9-10, 66-67, 83; German reports cited in footnote 10; France, UNEDIC, Bulletin de Liaison, March 1974, "Enquête sur le chômage des jeunes".

18. Figaro, June 4, 1975, "Lionel Stoleru: Tenir le seuil des 800,000 chômeurs".

19. New York Times, May 19, 1975, "Recession Kills Black Teen-Ager Hopes"; Blacks Link Job Woes to Employers' Racism"; May 4, 1975, "The Teen-age Worker is Hardest Hit"; Great Britain, Department of Employment, Final Triennial Report by the National Youth Employment Council", p. 23; Great Britain. Community Relations Commission, Unemployment and Homelessness: A Report, London: HMSO, 1974, pp. 41-44; New York Times, June 20, 1975, "Economy Held Key to Child Suicides".

20. New York Times, August 17, 1975, Business and Finance section, Robert Eisner, "A Way to Create Jobs: Cut Payroll Taxes".

21. OECD, Regional Seminar on Youth Unemployment, Country Report: Austria; Great Britain, Department of Employment, Unqualified, Untrained, Unemployed, p. 49.

22. Great Britain, <u>Department of Employment Gazette</u>, April 1975, p. 328.

23. Canada, Department of Manpower and Immigration, <u>Summary of statistical data from the Local Initiatives Programme</u>, 1972-73.

24. OECD, Manpower and Social Affairs Committee, "Interim Report of the Working Party on Employment", MO(75)3, p.5; Great Britain, Manpower Services Commission, <u>There's Work to be Done</u>, pp. 69-70.

25. <u>Manpower Report of the President</u>, 1975.

BIBLIOGRAPHY

National reports (1)

Australia - "The insertion of youth into working life: the Australian situation", report provided by the Australian Authorities, 1975.

Canada - "The Canadian perception of the entry process and its problems", by G.N. Perry, 1975.

Finland - "Entry into the labour market of young people who have finished their studies", by A. Pulkkinen, 1975.

France - "La qualification des emplois offerts aux jeunes gens et jeunes filles à la sortie du système éducatif français", by G. Ducray, 1975.

Germany - "Réponses actuelles au chômage des jeunes en Allemagne", report provided by the German Authorities, 1976.

Ireland - "The insertion of youth into working life: the Irish situation", by M.E.J. O'Kelly, 1975.

Italy - "Le passage de l'école à la vie professionnelle: la situation italienne", by F. Taiti, 1975.

Spain - "L'insertion des jeunes dans la vie professionnelle en Espagne", by R. de Cossio, 1975.

Sweden - "Insertion of youth into working life: the Swedish situation", by B. Ringholm, 1975.

Yugoslavia - "L'insertion des jeunes dans la vie professionnelle en Yougoslavie", by D. Tomasevic, 1975.

Reports and documents prepared by OECD (1)

"Youth and community services", by J.A.B. McLeish, 1975.

"Réflexions sur les rapports entre éducation et emploi dans une perspective italienne", by G. Martinoli, 1975.

"The place of the occupational component in education and training", by B.G. Reubens, 1975.

Beyond compulsory schooling: Options and changes in upper secondary education, 1976.

"New options in education and employment for young people. Experts' Group meeting, Paris, 3rd and 4th December, 1975".

"Summary record of a Meeting of Experts on the Entry of young people into working life held in Paris on 6th and 7th May, 1975".

1) To be published under the title: Entry of young people into Working Life - Technical Reports.

Other references

Barbagli, M. - Disoccupazione intellettuale e sistema scolastico in Italia, Bologna, II Mulino, 1974.

Barnagli, M. and others - Scuola e mercato del lavoro, Bologna, II Mulino, 1975.

Barton, P.A. - "Opportunity for careers", Washington, The Manpower Institute, 1974.

Bégué, J. - "La montée des emplois tertiaires", Paris, Economie et statistique, June 1969.

Berg, I - The great training robbery, New York, Praeger, 1970.

Briat, A.M. - "Métier, diplômes, représentations d'adolescents des 1er et 2ème cycles", Paris, L'orientation scolaire et profession-nelle, 1962, nr 2.

Carpentier, J. - "Organisational techniques and the humanisation of work", Geneva, International labour review, August 1974.

Coleman, J.S. and others - Youth, Transition to adulthood, Chicago Report of the Panel on youth of the President's Science advisory Committee, University of Chicago Press, 1974.

Diamond, D. and Bedrosian H. - Industry hiring requirements and employment of disadvantaged groups, New York, University School of commerce, 1970.

Doeringer, P. and Piore, M.J. - "Unemployment and the dual labor market", Public Interest, Winter 1974.

Dumazedier, J. and de Gisors, H. - "Réussite scolaire et insertion professionnelle", Paris, Orientations, July 1972.

Folk, H. - The problem of youth unemployment in the transition from school to work, Princeton, 1968.

Freedman, M. - The process of work establishment, New York, Columbia University Press, 1969.

Gavett, T. and others - Youth unemployment and minimum wages, U.S. Bureau of labor statistics, 1970.

Géminard, L. - "The pedagogical aspects of the 16-19 age group", in Janne H. and Géminard L., The educational needs of the 16-19 age group, Strasbourg, Standing Conference of European Ministers of education, eighth session, 1973.

Ginzberg, E. - "A critical look at career guidance", Manpower, February 1972.

Greenaway, H. and Williams, G. - Patterns of change in graduate employment, London, Society for research into higher education, 1973.

Kalachek, E. - The youth labor market, U.S. National manpower policy task force, 1969.

Magaut, J. - "Vrais et faux salaires", Paris, Problèmes économiques, April 1974.

Marland, S.P. - Career education now, Washington, 1971.

Métais, G. - "La situation actuelle de l'apprentissage", <u>Bulletin de l'Association des conseillers d'orientation de France</u>, September-October 1970.

Newman, F. and others - <u>Report on higher education</u>, U.S. Department of Health, education and welfare, 1971, and <u>The second Newman report</u>, National policy and higher education, 1973.

O'Toole, J. - <u>The reserve army of the underemployed: Monograph on career education</u>, U.S. Department of Health, Education and Welfare, 1975.

Pohl, R. and others - "Enquête formation-qualification profession-nelle de 1970", Paris, <u>Démographie et emploi</u>, nr 32.

Pohl, R. and others - "Enquête sur l'emploi de 1972", Paris, <u>Démographie et emploi</u>, nr 32-34.

Reubens, B. - "Vocational education for all in high school", in J. O'Toole, ed., <u>Work and the quality of life</u>, Cambridge, MIT, 1974.

Rousselet, J. - <u>L'allergie au travail</u>, Paris, 1974.

Seers, D. and others - <u>Matching employment, opportunities and expectations</u>, Geneva, International Labour Office, 1971.

Thurow, L. - "Education and economic equality", <u>The public interest</u>, Summer 1972.

Vincens, J. and Robinson, D. - <u>Research into Labour market behavior</u>, Paris, OECD, 1974.

Yankelovich, D. - <u>The changing values on campus: political and personal attitudes on campus</u>, New York, 1972.

<u>Educational statistics yearbook</u>, vol. I, International tables, Paris, OECD, 1974.

<u>Arbetskraftsundersökningen, 1965-1974</u> (Sweden), Statistiska Centralbyrån.

<u>Devenir professionnel des étudiants à la sortie des universités</u>, Paris, Centre d'études et de recherches sur les qualifications, Document nr 19, December 1973.

<u>L'accès à la vie professionnelle à la sortie des Instituts universi-taires de technologie</u>, Paris, Centre d'études et de recherches sur les qualifications, Dossier nr 7, June 1973.

<u>La situazione educativa del paese</u> (Italie), Rome, Quindicinale di note e commenti CENSIS, October 1973 and October 1975.

"Youth unemployment in the European Community", Brussels, Commission of the European Communities, Note of 21st January, 1976.

<u>Unemployment among young people and its social aspects</u>, Strasbourg, Council of Europe, 1972.

<u>Les attitudes des travailleurs et des employeurs à l'égard de l'em-ploi</u>, Paris, Cahiers du Centre d'études de l'emploi, 1973, nr 2.

<u>Les emplois tenus par les jeunes de 17 ans</u>, Paris, Centre d'études et de recherches sur les qualifications, Dossier nr 3, May 1972.

"Les étudiants jugent l'université", Générations, November 1973.

Les possibilités d'emploi selon les qualifications acquises dans les formations initiales, Paris, Centre d'études et de recherches sur les qualifications, Dossier nr 4, June 1972.

"L'opération Protechnique, Rapports de synthèse", Paris, Informations SIDA, July-August 1971.

Manpower report of the President 1974, U.S. Department of Labor, 1975.

"Measures to reduce youth unemployment", Bruxelles, Commission of the European Communities, Note of 6th May, 1975.

Educational policies for the seventies, General report of the Conference on policies for educational growth, Paris, OECD, 1971.

"Recommendations of the Council on a general employment and manpower policy", Meeting of the Manpower and Social affairs Committee at ministerial level, 4th to 5th March, 1976, Paris, OECD, 1976.

"Sviluppo della scolarità e mercato del lavoro" (Italie), Rome, Quindicinale di note e commenti CENSIS, April 1973.

Tableaux de l'Education nationale (France), Paris, Ministère de l'Education nationale (published yearly).

Work in America, Report of a Special task force to the Secretary of Health, Education and Welfare, Cambridge (Mass.), MIT, 1973.

OECD SALES AGENTS
DEPOSITAIRES DES PUBLICATIONS DE L'OCDE

ARGENTINA – ARGENTINE
Carlos Hirsch S.R.L.,
Florida 165, BUENOS-AIRES.
☎ 33-1787-2391 Y 30-7122
AUSTRALIA – AUSTRALIE
International B.C.N. Library Suppliers Pty Ltd.,
161 Sturt St., South MELBOURNE, Vic. 3205.
☎ 699-6388
658 Pittwater Road, BROOKVALE NSW 2100.
☎ 938 2267
AUSTRIA – AUTRICHE
Gerold and Co., Graben 31, WIEN 1. ☎ 52.22.35
BELGIUM – BELGIQUE
Librairie des Sciences
Coudenberg 76-78, B 1000 BRUXELLES 1.
☎ 512-05-60
BRAZIL – BRESIL
Mestre Jou S.A., Rua Guaipá 518,
Caixa Postal 24090, 05089 SAO PAULO 10.
☎ 261-1920
Rua Senador Dantas 19 s/205-6, RIO DE
JANEIRO GB. ☎ 232-07. 32
CANADA
Renouf Publishing Company Limited
2182 St. Catherine Street West
MONTREAL, Quebec H3H 1M7
☎ (514) 937-3519
DENMARK – DANEMARK
Munksgaards Boghandel
Nørregade 6, 1165 KØBENHAVN K.
☎ (01) 12 69 70
FINLAND – FINLANDE
Akateeminen Kirjakauppa
Keskuskatu 1, 00100 HELSINKI 10. ☎ 625.901
FRANCE
Bureau des Publications de l'OCDE
2 rue André-Pascal, 75775 PARIS CEDEX 16.
☎ 524.81.67
Principaux correspondants :
13602 AIX-EN-PROVENCE : Librairie de
l'Université. ☎ 26.18.08
38000 GRENOBLE : B. Arthaud. ☎ 87.25.11
GERMANY – ALLEMAGNE
Verlag Weltarchiv G.m.b.H.
D 2000 HAMBURG 36, Neuer Jungfernstieg 21
☎ 040-35-62-500
GREECE – GRECE
Librairie Kauffmann, 28 rue du Stade,
ATHENES 132. ☎ 322.21.60
HONG-KONG
Government Information Services,
Sales and Publications Office,
Beaconsfield House, 1st floor,
Queen's Road, Central
☎ H-233191
ICELAND – ISLANDE
Snaebjörn Jónsson and Co., h.f.,
Hafnarstraeti 4 and 9, P.O.B. 1131,
REYKJAVIK. ☎ 13133/14281/11936
INDIA – INDE
Oxford Book and Stationery Co. :
NEW DELHI, Scindia House. ☎ 45896
CALCUTTA, 17 Park Street. ☎ 240832
IRELAND – IRLANDE
Eason and Son, 40 Lower O'Connell Street,
P.O.B. 42, DUBLIN 1. ☎ 74 39 35
ISRAEL
Emanuel Brown :
35 Allenby Road, TEL AVIV. ☎ 51049/54082
also at :
9, Shlomzion Hamalka Street, JERUSALEM.
☎ 234807
48 Nahlath Benjamin Street, TEL AVIV.
☎ 53276
ITALY – ITALIE
Libreria Commissionaria Sansoni :
Via Lamarmora 45, 50121 FIRENZE. ☎ 579751
Via Bartolini 29, 20155 MILANO. ☎ 365083
Sous-dépositaires :
Editrice e Libreria Herder,
Piazza Montecitorio 120, 00186 ROMA.
☎ 674628
Libreria Hoepli, Via Hoepli 5, 20121 MILANO.
☎ 865446
Libreria Lattes, Via Garibaldi 3, 10122 TORINO.
☎ 519274
La diffusione delle edizioni OCDE è inoltre assicu-
rata dalle migliori librerie nelle città più importanti.

JAPAN – JAPON
OECD Publications Centre,
Akasaka Park Building,
2-3-4 Akasaka,
Minato-ku
TOKYO 107. ☎ 586-2016
KOREA – COREE
Pan Korea Book Corporation
P.O.Box n° 101 Kwangwhamun, SEOUL
☎ 72-7369
LEBANON – LIBAN
Documenta Scientifica/Redico
Edison Building, Bliss Street,
P.O.Box 5641, BEIRUT. ☎ 354429 – 344425
THE NETHERLANDS – PAYS-BAS
W.P. Van Stockum
Buitenhof 36, DEN HAAG. ☎ 070-65.68.08
NEW ZEALAND – NOUVELLE-ZELANDE
The Publications Manager,
Government Printing Office,
WELLINGTON: Mulgrave Street (Private Bag),
World Trade Centre, Cubacade, Cuba Street,
Rutherford House, Lambton Quay ☎ 737-320
AUCKLAND: Rutland Street (P.O.Box 5344)
☎ 32.919
CHRISTCHURCH : 130 Oxford Tce, (Private Bag)
☎ 50.331
HAMILTON : Barton Street (P.O.Box 857)
☎ 80.103
DUNEDIN : T & G Building, Princes Street
(P.O.Box 1104), ☎ 78.294
NORWAY – NORVEGE
Johan Grundt Tanums Bokhandel,
Karl Johansgate 41/43, OSLO 1. ☎ 02-332980
PAKISTAN
Mirza Book Agency, 65 Shahrah Quaid-E-Azam,
LAHORE 3. ☎ 66839
PHILIPPINES
R.M. Garcia Publishing House,
903 Quezon Blvd. Ext., QUEZON CITY,
P.O. Box 1860 – MANILA. ☎ 99.98.47
PORTUGAL
Livraria Portugal,
Rua do Carmo 70-74. LISBOA 2. ☎ 360582/3
SPAIN – ESPAGNE
Mundi-Prensa Libros, S.A.
Castelló 37, Apartado 1223, MADRID-1. ☎ 275.46.55
Libreria Bastinos
Pelayo, 52, BARCELONA 1. ☎ 222.06.00
SWEDEN – SUEDE
Fritzes Kungl. Hovbokhandel,
Fredsgatan 2, 11152 STOCKHOLM 16.
☎ 08/23 89 00
SWITZERLAND – SUISSE
Librairie Payot, 6 rue Grenus, 1211 GENEVE 11.
☎ 022-31.89.50
TAIWAN – FORMOSE
National Book Company
84-5 Sing Sung Rd., Sec. 3
TAIPEI 107. ☎ 321-0698
TURKEY – TURQUIE
Librairie Hachette,
469 Istiklal Caddesi,
Beyoglu, ISTANBUL, ☎ 44.94.70
et 14 E Ziya Gökalp Caddesi
ANKARA. ☎ 12.10.80
UNITED KINGDOM – ROYAUME-UNI
H.M. Stationery Office, P.O.B. 569, LONDON
SE1 9 NH, ☎ 01-928-6977, Ext. 410
or
49 High Holborn
LONDON WC1V 6HB (personal callers)
Branches at: EDINBURGH, BIRMINGHAM,
BRISTOL, MANCHESTER, CARDIFF.
BELFAST.
UNITED STATES OF AMERICA
OECD Publications Center, Suite 1207,
1750 Pennsylvania Ave, N.W.
WASHINGTON, D.C. 20006. ☎ (202)298-8755
VENEZUELA
Libreria del Este, Avda. F. Miranda 52,
Edificio Galipán, Aptdo. 60 337, CARACAS 106.
☎ 32 23 01/33 26 04/33 24 73
YUGOSLAVIA – YOUGOSLAVIE
Jugoslovenska Knjiga, Terazije 27, P.O.B. 36,
BEOGRAD. ☎ 621-992

Les commandes provenant de pays où l'OCDE n'a pas encore désigné de dépositaire peuvent être adressées à :
OCDE, Bureau des Publications, 2 rue André-Pascal, 75775 Paris CEDEX 16
Orders and inquiries from countries where sales agents have not yet been appointed may be sent to
OECD, Publications Office, 2 rue André-Pascal, 75775 Paris CEDEX 16

OECD PUBLICATIONS, 2, rue André-Pascal, 75775 Paris Cedex 16 - No. 38 939 1977

PRINTED IN FRANCE